4 - 2

4-2

David Thomson

BLOOMSBURY

First published in Great Britain 1996
The paperback edition published in 1997
Bloomsbury Publishing Plc, 38 Soho Square, London W1V 5DF

Copyright © David Thomson

The moral right of the author has been asserted

A CIP record for this book is available from the British Library

ISBN 0 7475 3091 2

10 9 8 7 6 5 4 3 2 1

Printed by Cox and Wyman Ltd, Reading

Contents

For Kate, Mathew, Rachel, Nicholas and Zachary,
and for Alistair Cooke

RULES OF THE GAME

There are the rules, and what we make of them. It's the same with soccer and writing a book; with playing jazz or getting through the week. You've got to keep the ball on the island and the words on the page; and you've got to stay within the rules, or woo them till they bend.

The page and the island are prisons if you want to think of them that way, and there are real prisons where a certain genius can go wild: Jean Genet in how ever many cubic feet, and Charlie Parker in just the bars allowed by 'How High the Moon'.

The week was like that in those days: for between the dutiful finishing of Friday and the fixed purgatory of the Sunday that John Osborne railed against there was the jazzy liberty of Saturday. Greatest day in the week, though with any day that good how did the English let Sundays stay dead so long?

As well as movies, I loved jazz and soccer in those days – this is around 1963, I am talking about. And I realize now that if I'm going to write about this, then I have to try to spell out their resemblance. It's not enough to note the strict forms, the rules, and the internal, imprisoned chance of taking off on the spur, of improvising, of setting off towards one's own goal, only to lull the defence into rash positions that a swift turn will expose. It is all of that, but it is also the air of sailing along on the moment, borne on the rhythm, sure of one's technique, but serene too in the hope that some new line will be found and followed.

That very basic soccer urge – I tap it to my left, sway that way, sympathetically, and then reer back to the right – is there too in jazz in the elemental asking and answering of spontaneous phrases. It is the balance that ensures headlong motion will not fall over. It swings, as Jimmy McIlroy and Denis Law swung, just as much as Ben Webster or Art Pepper.

Jazz was American; as well as movies, it was reason for loving that country. Of course, there were some very good British jazz musicians – George Chisholm, Tubby Hayes, Stan Tracey – but to follow jazz in those days meant waiting for the tours by people and bands you might never ever see more than once in your life. I saw Miles Davis, for about twelve minutes, before he lost interest in the evening. I saw Lena Horne command the Palladium. And I saw the Ellington orchestra, all those muted dandies. And once – I think it was at the Davis in Croydon – I saw Louis Armstrong. And then after the show, I walked around that huge building, and there on a back street a door opened and Louis was there, feet away, saying goodbye to a lady. You could feel the warmth coming off him, like sweat and true feeling.

But then, in 1963 – a key year in so many ways, as you will see in this story about 1966 – something changed. Rock and roll was all very well and as British as the Beatles, thank you. But around that time, in pubs and clubs in Richmond and south London, where I lived, people my age started playing jazz on guitars. It was rhythm and blues; it was American. It was so authentic for a few years and so good that people like Jimi Hendrix had to come to England to be themselves. It was John Mayall, the Yardbirds, Eric Clapton, Jeff Beck, Alexis Korner, and so on. In all my life I don't think I've known a more complete or loving appropriation of America by the British than that – and it led to Mick Jagger sounding as black as my hair was then.

This is a kind of introduction to say that this is a soccer book about many other things, all of which were expressed in soccer. And about a day in July 1966 that a generation is always replaying, and which means as much to me now, writing from America, as that gentle, wise voice in my growing up, Alistair Cooke in his letters from America. This book is dedicated to Mr Cooke, and his bridging the Atlantic – if he will share with my favourite starting forward line.

FIRST HALF

1

'This is the day we've all been waiting for,' says Kenneth Wolstenholme at the start of the BBC match commentary. And yet you know how dodgy such days can be – we could win, we might lose; we could be getting happily married or entering into a life of helpless, bitter silence; this could be the start of your future, or the beginning of the end. At five to three in the afternoon you wouldn't mind if the day we've all been waiting for was one more day of peace and rest and ease away. After all, the waiting can be a cracker. Wasn't waiting for Christmas better than the day itself, even if the waiting left you sick to your stomach?

But this is five to three, or maybe seven or eight minutes to three, on the afternoon of Saturday July 30th 1966. Match day: Saturday. And the lads are there in a fidgeting line in the gloom of the tunnel, behind Alf Ramsey, waiting to come out, four of them are bouncing balls and the others are doing all those little things short of screaming or really getting into the space of the West German team who are in their own line a couple of steps away.

England are in red shirts – cherry red – full-sleeved, with a simple, rounded neck; white shorts; red socks. West Germany are in white shirts, short-sleeved, with a thick black ring at the ends of the sleeves and at the neck; black shorts, white socks. Compared with the fantastical, hideous gear players wear now

(1995–96), heavy with badges, logos, trade marks and sponsored crests, these 1966 teams look classical and modern. It's as if football kit never got any simpler or better. And England in that unfamiliar, passionate red are an image we will never lose. Germany had the first option on white, so England changed, all for the sake of the black-and-white TV. But God knows why every England team ever afterwards didn't lock down that red as the eternal style.

There are eleven of them in the line: Bobby Moore, George Cohen, Alan Ball, Gordon Banks, Roger Hunt, Ray Wilson, Geoff Hurst, Bobby Charlton, Martin Peters, Nobby Stiles and Jack Charlton at the back. Maybe it wasn't the best team. We can argue over that. Maybe it wasn't the most glorious team England's ever had. But selection is just like casting: out of all the indecision and the lost nerve that can't make a choice, Vivien Leigh becomes Scarlett O'Hara. Owns it. So these lads *are* the team, for ever, the best remembered, those noble reds who had got to the Final itself, the Final of the World Cup, and were about to see whether they could go further still, even as far as eternity, on the day we had all been waiting for.

Not everyone has made it to the Saturday, even if they had known what the waiting was for. On the previous Saturday, the 23rd, as England had just survived in what everyone, for many reasons, regarded as the 'disgraceful' quarter-final match with Argentina, Montgomery Clift had died in New York. 'Suddenly' the papers said: he was only forty-five. But those close to him – as we know now – had only wondered *when* it was going to happen, and when the gaunt, broken man was going to yield to paranoia, booze, his bag of drugs and his essential instability. He was being looked after, with desperate fondness, but he kept on telling his friend Lorenzo that he resembled the Dirk Bogarde character in that English film, *The Servant*, in which the malicious manservant destroys the master.

Clift is an aside, but not a digression. As Matthew Garth, the lean, dark, laconic adopted son to John Wayne in *Red River*, he was the first hero I remember having. I had named my son Mathew, born twenty-one months before that Saturday July 30th, because of *Red River*. I had followed Clift's career, believed in him as an actor, and cherished him as an icon. And this is a book about heroes and our worship of them. Clift's Garth had the natural subtlety and the rather veiled lethal air of a great inside-forward. The way he talked back to Wayne, say, you could see that attitude working with Finney and Matthews on his wings, and Tommy Lawton and Wilf Mannion there to snap up the chances.

So Clift's death was a very noticeable drag on the build-up towards Final day. Then on Monday the 25th, Tony Lema – such an easy golfer, such a relaxed man, it seemed, 'Champagne' Tony Lema – was killed in a plane crash. In the several days after July 30th, the day we had all been waiting for, but which couldn't help being followed by other days, Bud Powell and Lenny Bruce died. Like Clift, they were only in their forties, and they had only themselves to blame and the choices they had made of what to put into their bodies. Chances are that Clift, Powell and Bruce knew nothing and cared less about the match, but I knew them, and I knew that a Bud Powell solo, or a Bruce riff, was in the same nature of flight and wonder as Denis Law or Ferenc Puskas going off on a rapture with a football. In 1966, I'd have sworn by Clift and Powell, and I felt that Lema and Bruce were rare geniuses – four Americans – so it was a bad time, too.

There they are, the English team, coming out of the tunnel, into the roaring light of English support and a day that is so poker-faced. The weather forecast said 'sunny periods and showers, heavy and thundery at times and with hail in places, becoming mainly dry and clear later'. By three in the afternoon, only the hail was lacking, in Isleworth, on Bridge Road, in a two-down, three-up, semi-detached house, purchased two years before at £4,250, opposite the allotments, where I lived with my wife, Anne, with Kate, who was five, Mathew, and Rachel, who was coming up on three months. I watched the game there on television with Mathew on my lap, when he was patient or tired enough to stay there, and my father was, I suppose, watching on his television set in a very similar shaped house in Park Street, near St Albans. I never spoke to him that day; I didn't know the phone number then.

He was fifty-seven; I was twenty-five. And our England was . . . well, to be brief about it for this moment, our England, our United Kingdom, was in the best of times and the worst. There was Harold Wilson's Labour government, re-elected that March 31st with an improved majority of 97 seats – full of new ideas, urgent to make amends for 'thirteen years of Tory mis-rule', ablaze with the 'white heat of technology', and with Harold himself, puffing on his pipe, sly, chipper, dry, cocksure, smart, too smart maybe, but with the brisk air of a north-country manager saying it would all be OK so long as no-one forgot common sense. Unemployment was around half a million. The pound was 'down' to only $2.78. And there was an enormous economic crisis, greater than the public understood, or Wilson would admit to himself. Britain's gold and currency reserves had dropped by $372 million in four months. The trade gap widened by $67 million in June. Wilson's government had just called for a one-year freeze in pay, prices and dividends. It was uncertain whether they could ensure support from the trade unions. A holiday-maker going out of the country could take no more than £50 a year!

In America, it was another summer of racial strife in the big cities. In Cleveland, cops had stood by helplessly as people looted stores. The indignation of blacks about their life was beginning to merge with the disquiet at the open-ended nature of the warfare in Vietnam. But in Saigon, Marshal Ky, the then leader of South Vietnam, had called for an invasion of the north or a twenty-year delay before that allegedly rotting nation fell of its own accord.

Britain was nearly bankrupt: today, historians are certain that Wilson should have devalued the pound that summer. But he was afraid, and hopeful: devaluation had been a mark of discredit and ignominy for Attlee's Labour government. So Harold gambled and made things worse.

Yet things were also better, or so much more fun, in Britain. In 1965, the death penalty had been abandoned. In 1966, the day before the Final, the report was issued of a group appointed by the Archbishop of Canterbury to look into divorce. It asserted the belief that divorce should have only one ground: irretrievable breakdown of the marriage – the erasure of blame or guilt. By 1967, the country admitted the legality of abortion and of homosexual behaviour between consenting adults.

Of course, there were those confident that every one of those advances was wrong and damaging. But the process of change was already under way, and in the mid-60s the necessary freshness of the liberties seemed bracing. That young energy was irresistible: it was using the birth control pill and the IUD (both of recent provision); it was driving hemlines up; it was using marijuana, like brandy, after dinner parties; it was fucking around. Was there more sex? Probably. Was the sex greeted with more insistence on pleasure? Certainly. There was a new, young, cool, hip style – it was to be seen in clothes, architecture, decor, haircuts and, above all, in the droll, insolent news conferences and the sweet harmonies of the Beatles. That foursome was as potent as any 4 in 4–2–4 or 4–3–3 on the soccer field. I am saying this quickly, here; but the Beatles were a team that affected English self-esteem that day at Wembley. Those Liverpool lads had pioneered world-beating in advance of Bill Shankly's team. But Anfield and Liverpool's success in the years ahead were given something greater than voice or heart by the Beatles.

Whether it was Beatle-ism, or Mersey Mania; Mary Quant and Carnaby Street; or just that air of placid readiness in young English women – *Time* magazine was stirred enough to identify a thing it called 'swinging London'.

Soccer players didn't have the nerve yet to look like Beatles or come on like swingers. Actually, the Beatles themselves were still rather close-trimmed, and plainly provincials just getting used to having London at their feet. They still believed in doing big international tours. But they couldn't hear themselves play, and they heard their remarks – the wry jokes and the stringent observations – go mad in the echo-chamber of celebrity. John Lennon had reckoned in a matter-of-fact way to Maureen Cleave of the *Evening Standard* that the Beatles now were likely bigger than Jesus Christ. And suddenly the world wasn't that hip or cool; millions said they were outraged by such sacrilege. The Beatles weren't too far from neurosis. They would play their last ever concert at the end of that summer, in San Francisco, at Candlestick Park, a place where I was headed, had I but dreamed of it.

On that Saturday, though, I felt absolutely, perfectly happy – granted I couldn't endure the thought of losing to West Germany – stuck in Isleworth, with the game to see. That morning the bookies called it 7–4 on England, 11–8 against West Germany. £5 seats were being scalped for £20. The ten-shilling standing tickets were fetching £6 15s. On the Friday, Harold Wilson had been in Washington, meeting with Lyndon Johnson. He had wanted help from America, and hadn't got much, so he came out of the meeting and said it had been a very useful exchange of information. Otherwise, he trusted 'the unshakable resolve of the British Government and people to right the people's difficulties'.

There was news of mutiny in the Nigerian army. Processions were being banned in Belfast. The movies in London included *Khartoum*, *Who's Afraid of Virginia Woolf?*, *Arabesque*, *Doctor Zhivago* (still, a year after its opening), *Nevada Smith* and *Walk, Don't Run*, Cary Grant's farewell performance. In the theatre, you could see Anna Neagle in *Charlie Girl*, Fenella Fielding in *Let's Get a Divorce*, Dora Bryan in *Hello, Dolly!*, Honor Blackman in *Wait Until Dark*, Hermione Baddeley in *The Killing of Sister George* and Vanessa Redgrave in *The Prime of Miss Jean Brodie*.

There was racing at Epsom, Newcastle, Thirsk and Warwick. Surrey entertained Essex at the Oval, and Gary Sobers's great

West Indies team would be playing Glamorgan at Swansea. The Queen and the Duke of Edinburgh would be at the Final. And Harold Wilson would be there beside them. There he is. He flew back from America through the night, landed at Heathrow at 1.30 p. m. and had a car waiting to take him to Wembley (before the M25).

It is five to three on this terrific, sullen, pregnant afternoon. My son Mathew is twenty-one months. The wife I have now, as I write, Lucy, was eleven. David Platt was seven weeks old. Paul Ince, Alan Shearer, Paul Gascoigne – they are not born yet. But England are coming out on to the field and their tense legs feel the great thickness and lush spread of that summer pasture that has been rained upon for days.

Three o'clock, Saturday July 30th 1966, for ever.

2

The nervousness of the players does all it can to hustle the Royal Marine band off the pitch. They have been there dutifully plugging through tunes associated with the last sixteen nations in the Cup. Swinging London has not yet got a full sense of showmanship. The national anthems of the enemies from two wars are more the Marines' cup of tea. And the crowd – maybe ten Englishmen to one German – sings lustily and piously. Yes, the wars are there as an undertone, but that is not a fear. The fear is that the wondrous and unbearable occasion is upon us.

Then the Swiss referee, Gottfried Dienst – German-speaking – supervises the meeting of skippers Bobby Moore and Uwe Seeler. Seeler gives Moore a pennant; the German gets a plaque. The coin is exhibited. It goes up in the air and England wins. Moore elects to defend the goal England has picked for the warm-up. The spare balls are kicked away – the last carefree kicks of the day – and the two teams fall into their line-ups, the trenchification of 4–3–3:

Gordon Banks

George Cohen   Bobby Moore   Jack Charlton   Ray Wilson

Nobby Stiles   Alan Ball   Martin Peters

Roger Hunt   Bobby Charlton   Geoff Hurst

O

Lothar Emmerich   Siegfried Held   Uwe Seeler

Wolfgang Overath   Franz Beckenbauer   Helmut Haller

Karl-Heinz   Wolfgang Weber   Willy Schulz   Horst-Dieter
Schnellinger   Höttges

Hans Tilkowski

There are no substitutes in these days. If a player is hurt, he must do his best or get off the pitch. Nor can anyone out of form be replaced. In the earlier match, Brazil v. Portugal, the great Pelé had been injured early on and remained as just a limping passenger. Football then, you may conclude, is still a man's game: injury and hurt are to be borne bravely. And Wembley has its tales of injured heroes. That rich ground has held too many studs, so turning knees and ankles give way in agony. In the 1953 Cup Final, Bolton Wanderers v. Blackpool – the Stanley Matthews final – Bolton's Eric Bell was badly injured. He spent the game hobbling around, but then there he was to get Bolton's third goal – 3–1 – so that Stanley had to work a little bit of magic on the right wing before Blackpool could get their (and his) victory.

No substitutes means something else: no Greaves. The great and much beloved imp, Jimmy, will not have a chance at a rescue act. Ramsey has declined to pick him, not that unkindly, but firmly and philosophically and as if from a distance, without taking him aside and talking to him. So, on the face of it, Geoff Hurst is there in Greaves's place; though, after fifteen minutes of the game, you'd reckon it was Roger Hunt who edged him, the

Roger Hunt who can muster hardly a class moment in the match. Jimmy pulling up his shorts would have been more exciting. But more of this anon.

Herr Dienst blows his whistle. Held taps the ball forward and Overath stops it, steadies, and sends an elegant left-foot ball across the pitch to his right and out of play. Haller, who looks heavy, is yards too slow to get to it. Is this just tension, or does Germany mean to attack on the right?

Peters takes the throw in, and puts it neatly at Bobby Moore's feet. Moore has ample space: there's no early sign of dogged marking. But Bobby sends a pass forward in the air to Hurst (who is plainly ready to flick it off to someone else) when he is brusquely challenged by Höttges from behind.

Free kick. Wilson prepares to take it, and Moore is rolling up quietly behind him and to his left. The kick is stroked on those few yards to Bobby, and as he takes it to the sideline he is threatened by Haller. Bobby is never going to be quick – but it is his grace not to need to be. So he lays it off again back to Ray Wilson (they are at the half-way line), and as Haller carries his challenge on to the back so Wilson slides the ball up the touchline to Peters.

This is the first pretty move of the game. Peters touches it inside to Bobby Charlton who does that lovely inside turn he has, making the lagging pass seem made for his measure. There are small things Bobby does in midfield that make you cherish him. He then lays it off in front of the advancing Stiles – thirty yards from goal, say – and, even if he didn't mean to do so, the crowd's mounting roar determines that he will shoot.

The ball is deflected away by a defender, to the England right. Cohen, coming up, full steam, jumps for it. But he is all wrong in timing and it is all he can do to touch the ball as it passes by. A German gathers it by the touchline (Schulz?), and passes it inside to Beckenbauer who does a reverse turn (rather like Charlton's seconds ago) to control the ball and a bit of space. Beckenbauer is twenty – the youngest man on the field – and plainly a danger. He begins to make a triangle with Overath, but that player's pass is deflected and so it comes to Cohen (who has got back very quickly).

Cohen calms the ball and gives it sideways to Moore, and so for the second time already Bobby makes a good pass forward to Hurst, who lays it off to Peters. He takes it deftly inside the referee and, exploiting that decoy, has a few yards of space, going forward on those long, thin-legged strides. He has real opportunity, but then he palpably pauses – as if confounded or intimidated by the glimpse of power. It is enough for Seeler to be at him, so that Peters's shot is deflected, high but slow, the momentum lost. Bobby Charlton has been moving forward to get it, but Weber knocks it clear. It comes back to Peters who can do nothing but take a snap volley shot. He tries, but he is a tad slow, and not strong enough to dominate a ball heavy with spin. The shot goes high and wide. Goal-kick.

The crowd groans and sways back – there is nothing now but slaughter and goals that will appease them. They move towards and away from the action in great digestive convulsions as tight-packed limbs on the terraces feel the need to kick and run. Such standing crowds as these are no more – for safety's sake – but you must imagine what they were like.

'Blimey, mate,' says the stranger beside me. 'You going to go through every single move?'

'I haven't made up my mind yet,' I tell him.

'We'll be here years,' he says.

'We have been already,' I answer. 'Thirty years later and you and I are still watching this match. We know the result. We know what happens. But we're watching it as if it's all new.'

I can see that this has dispirited him a little, so I try to make amends.

'England are looking useful,' I suggest.

'Very nice, mate, very nice. You got your West Ham boys in synch early. Gerry looks panicky.'

There's that hint of the war – how many movies have a line

like that? 'Gerry's a bit edgy tonight, sir.' 'Is he, number one, well, let's give him something to worry about, shall we?' 'Hoping you'd say that, sir! The cold porridge?' 'Exactly, number one.'

England are looking *good*, or trim. There have been enough accurate, thoughtful ground passes, with movement off the ball in anticipation, to remind ourselves of what Ramsey has accomplished. He is a very good manager at getting loyalists to do the sensible thing tidily, and he has a way of making those things fit what his players are capable of. He likes honest effort and sound skills that disdain experiment or brilliance. You possess the football with Alf for long enough until you see an opening or a mistake in your opponent. It's a system that depends on complete fitness and obedience.

'Our Jimmy might have put that one in,' says my new friend.

'Chelsea supporter?' I ask.

'Spurs!' he says, a mite indignant.

'He was ours before he was yours,' I say, remembering that glum time when it was clear that Greaves was leaving Chelsea.

You see, there's a history to that World Cup of 1966, as well as an aftermath. As soon as I say that, I see a picture from England v. Hungary, at Wembley, in 1953. It's a shot from behind and to one side of the goal. Our rather ridiculously dapper and moustached goalkeeper, Gil Merrick (he sounds like a heel in a Joan Crawford movie, and he looked like Zachary Scott in *Mildred Pierce*), has somehow tipped a shot round the post – though the look on his face seems to wonder if it isn't going in. But there, seen through the netting, is the English right back – Alf Ramsey himself – his Brylcreem black hair parted in the middle, the long sleeves rolled up on his loose white shirt (it has a proper collar, too), and his baggy black shorts the helpless companions to an instinctive, yet sheepish, jeté he has made, as if yearning to kick the ball clear. The look on Ramsey's face is stricken, grim and sombre.

Why not? That November, mid-week afternoon, Hungary came to Wembley and beat us 6–3. No, thrashed us; it could have been 10–3 (six months later, in Budapest, it was 7–1).

Before the kick-off, two of the Hungarians – Puskas and Kocsis – chose to do ball tricks in the centre circle – rolling it on their thighs, juggling, bravura stuff. It was showing off, and some of the English players may have sneered at such 'Continental stuff', but it was a warning, too. For those two were demonstrating a kind of close ball control that only one of the English players – Matthews – might have matched. Except, he'd learned to be ashamed of it: years had taught Stanley to dim his own brilliance.

England then had no ideal centre-half, yet in those days the English method depended on a big, strong, not unduly gentle stopper at the heart of the defence. Not just to break up attacks and rule the air, but to give the other defenders confidence. Neil Franklin had been that man for years after the war, but he was past it now and England were trying wing-halves, like Harry Johnston. He had Billy Wright and Jimmy Dickinson beside him, and Ramsey who was winning his thirty-second England cap – and his last.

Ramsey was slow, and set in his attitude. But he had been a very accomplished back – sound – a man ready to set up attacks and a cool taker of penalty kicks. Then the whole English defence was exposed and cut up by a Hungarian attack that roamed and switched, that harnessed ball tricks to larger, cunning designs, and that expected every player to have a killer finish as well as the capacity to go down a wing, unravelling the opposition: Puskas, Kocsis, Hidegkuti, Boszik and Czibor, a natural winger who piled the misery on Alf.

It was a very great day for football, as well as Hungary, and plenty of people in Britain learned the lesson. Which was that there was a kind of game to be played above and beyond the limited strategies and harsh contact of British soccer. 6–3 at Wembley was very important, and far harder to shrug off than the weird disaster of the 1950 World Cup. For in that competition – the first that England, the 'inventors' of the game, had ever deigned to enter – played in Brazil, the English team had a match, up country, at Belo Horizonte, against the USA.

Everyone in England knew the USA didn't play football, and indeed the US team came from some strange, obscure quarters. The English team was pretty good, as we thought: Bert Williams (a fine keeper), Ramsey and Aston as full-backs, Wright, Hughes and Dickinson as half-backs, and a forward line of Finney, Mannion, Bentley, Mortensen and Mullen. Stanley Matthews was in the team group, and any other country would have played him and Tom Finney on the wings without a second thought. We were beaten 1–0, and the blame went to a bumpy pitch, unreliable officiating (that eternal grumble for English soccer fans, and proof of foreign unsoundness) and the sheer, daft vagary of things. It was laughed off. We agreed to be good, wry losers. After all, it was only the World Cup. And in far-off Brazil.

Whereas, England had *never* been beaten by a foreign team at Wembley. Hungary played 4–2–4 and we were stuck with 2–3–5, because it had always worked, because it was the way football was played, wasn't it? and because it told players where they should be. In fact, the Hungarian formation changed all the time, whereas the shape of England could be read from the stands like a bomber formation. What could England do if Hidegkuti, the Hungarian centre-forward, played deep, away from our centre-half? The Hungarians used the spaces off the ball – they saw a game not just of kicking and heading, but slipping into unexpected positions. They controlled the ball and laid it off in a single motion. They played possession, and they ruled the midfield. Ramsey, afterwards, was quoted as saying it had all been a bit unfair. After all, four of their goals had been scored from outside the penalty area! Which allowed for Gil Merrick's forlorn, elegant dives.

3

Our Saturday afternoon at Wembley then goes into a doldrums that could as easily be Torquay v. Walsall in front of 3,514 people. In a matter of three or four minutes there are a dozen attacks, first one way, then the other, that are so filled with basic error and absent-mindedness the crowd sinks into one of those sours of boredom – just five minutes into the hour and a half they've all been waiting for. The German goal-kick prompts Schnellinger into a sixty-yard boot-away that Moore easily collects. He slips it forward to Ball, whose quick pass on to Hunt lets that handsome fellow side-foot the ball four yards to the left, and straight out of play. There's a round of booing at Hunt's neat, pathetic and evidently numb action. Why shouldn't there be players out there as scared as the fans? Just needing to get a first touch so they can be sure their feet won't fall off.

Schnellinger takes the throw-in and Schulz moves in on it to send a high ball downfield to Emmerich. Bobby Moore beats him in the air, but Emmerich picks up a rebound, turns, and rams a pass straight into Held's stomach as he stands on the edge of the box. The ball flops down and Held has a couple of steps of space on either side of him. It's a fat chance, but he turns and shoots wide. As the English fans regain their assurance, they hardly notice that the referee had blown for an offence. Did Held's hand help the ball to fall at his feet? We'll never know, or forget that he was open in a dangerous spot in front of goal.

The English back four want to play in a tidy line across the field, but Held has moved inside and somehow lost his marker.

Banks kicks away, but the ball comes straight back and now Held is racing with it down the left, just like a winger. Cohen goes with him, slips, recovers, but still can't stop Held putting in a cross from the goal line. It is cleared, but twice now Held has looked dangerous.

On the next English attack, Hurst is robbed by three Germans in midfield. Then the Germans are coming down the left flank again, but this time it's Emmerich and Haller with Seeler closing in on the cross until Jack Charlton knocks it sideways out of play. The throw-in goes to Schnellinger, who seems ready to back up these left-wing attacks, but then Schnellinger puts in a vague, lofted cross that ends up on the far side of the penalty area where Moore has plenty of time to gather it and release Bobby Charlton up the left, only for his pass on to go astray.

Höttges picks it up and then, somehow, walks the ball out of play. Bobby Charlton takes the throw-in. Ball gives it back to him and Bobby makes a sweet crossfield pass to Stiles breaking out of midfield, with yards all around him, room for a garden. Stiles is moving on goal and he gives what everyone else sees as a wall pass to Hunt. But, instead of laying it back to Stiles, Hunt goes off on a lateral amble and is easily dispossessed. One touch back and Stiles would have been set up for a shot.

The German possession gives it to Seeler, dropping deep, and he sends it out to Held, operating as a left-winger again. Held can't go round the defence, so he turns and pulls the ball back to Emmerich. But it comes to his weak, right foot. Emmerich's shot curves away absurdly so that it crosses the goal-line near the corner flag.

'They're looking handy down the left,' says my friend. Even in the dense standing crowd, he rolls his own cigarettes and a crooked twig of white flickers in his mouth as he talks.

'They've got three natural left-footers,' I say – meaning Held, Emmerich and Overath. 'Play to your strength.'

'That's the thing with the no-winger business,' he says. 'Your Ramsey does without wingers. So then the people he picks go down the wings. Stands to reason: fold 'em up round the edges. But full-backs don't have winger instincts, do they?'

My new friend has wisdom on his side. Alf Ramsey, the England team manager, has laboured towards the conclusion that England lacks wingers good enough at the international level. Since taking over as manager, in 1963, Ramsey has used traditional wingers like Terry Paine, Peter Thompson, John Connelly and Ian Callaghan. All except Thompson were actually chosen for the World Cup 22 and all three had one game in the qualifying round. Added to which, Bobby Charlton had often been selected as, or found himself gravitating towards, left wing. But Bobby could move inside so naturally, and he was often at his most dangerous when making a lateral or diagonal run and shooting on the pivot. But, then, why shouldn't wingers be free to cut inside – or even go to the opposite wing? The most dazzling player in English football – George Best of Northern Ireland – did that. As a matter of fact, his team, Manchester United, delighted in positional switching in those early to mid-1960s.

Take the United Team that won the First Division in '64–65. They had a forward line of Connelly, Law, Herd, Charlton, Best. Herd was the ostensible centre-forward, and he scored 22 goals, but Law had 28, Connelly 15, with Charlton and Best at 10 each. No-one ever knew where it was coming from. And there wasn't one of the five forwards – five, flat-out attackers, mind you – who couldn't pop up anywhere. Ramsey said we didn't have the wingers – like Matthews and Finney. But not playing wingers ran the risk of leaving those gorgeous wing spaces empty and asking Cohen and Wilson to think like raiders instead of guardians.

I remember the very first big game I ever saw. It was Blackpool v. Chelsea at the Bridge in February 1951. Maybe my Dad had taken me there for my tenth birthday. And I was being brought to witness Stanley Matthews, who was thirty-six then, so it was reckoned he would retire soon. I was going to see him before it was too late. (As it happened, I was still seeing him confront Chelsea when he was fifty.)

Chelsea then had a big double-decker stand at a corner of the ground that happened to look down on one of the right-wing spaces. We had seats there, and I remember the recurring sight of Matthews, his tangerine shirt flapping, bringing the ball up to the forlorn Chelsea left back, Bill Hughes, and taking it round him, past him, through him, in and out of him. Hughes was eviscerated, or made into a ghost; you could have thrown the towel in for him. But I don't remember him once fouling the frail-looking Matthews or other Chelsea defenders coming to his rescue. There seemed to be some general agreement that Stanley must be allowed to do his thing which was, quite simply, though with infinite variety, beating his man with the ball and moving forward. No one did it better. I don't know who won that game. But even at ten, high up in the stand, I could see that balance, control and mastery might be more lasting than any result.

Chelsea felt packed that day. And this was a time of huge crowds. For more than half its perimeter, Stamford Bridge then had terracing that must have gone thirty or forty concrete steps deep. The crowd record then was 82,905 for a game against Arsenal in 1935. Then there had been the November 1945 match against the touring Moscow Dynamo team – a goodwill gesture, and the first game I was ever told about. Some 74,000 paid admission that day, but there was chaos, so that people were getting in without paying, and everyone eager to see real Russians playing! Chelsea had a huge area then between the pitch and the crowd – enough for a running track and greyhound circle – and the people spilled on to these areas. They were all the way up to the goal line. Reports say there were 100,000 there to see the 3–3 draw, which included goals for Len Goulden and Tommy Lawton.

Tommy Lawton! My father said Lawton had a shot that was a 'rasper'. He demonstrated it in the games we played in the kitchen as my mother washed up. Our ball was soft and fluffy, a child's toy, and the goal was the legs of the kitchen table. My father helped me cut pictures of Tommy Lawton – aloft, alive, rasping – out of the newspapers. We stuck them in a book: I still have the sweet smell of the paste we used and the feeling of it, dry on my fingertips.

Well, that day, in 1951, when I had seen what a winger could do, I remember us leaving the ground. It was a prolonged ordeal. Then as now, the Bridge had only one exit, out on to the Fulham Road. It's always been a dangerous bottleneck, but there may have been 65,000 there that day to see Stanley, and I was ten. My father shielded me from the crunch and gripped my coat in the crush so I wouldn't fall. 'All right, lad,' he kept saying. And other men would call out, 'Nipper here! Nipper here!' So that people would do their best to hold back. I saw the faces of other kids, too, like the faces of children in Fagin's house in *Oliver Twist*. And as we inched forward, we passed the dog kennels – there would be racing that evening. And you could smell the dog shit as the animals got more and more excited by this great crowd. I thought I might be sick. But there was never any trouble. Apart from waiting hours to get a seat on a 49 bus home. My father said not to bother. We went off to a restaurant and had dinner to let the crowds go away. I'd never been to a restaurant before.

'Sounds like you had a good Dad, then,' says my friend.

Before I can answer, he's off again. 'Mine was a prince. Took me to the Spurs every home game. Len Duquemin, Ted Ditchburn, Ron Burgess, Bill Nicholson, and your Ramsey. Second Division Champions we were then – never looked back. Arthur Rowe was manager. He let 'em play – push and run. Good clean passing, very fast. We used to go every Saturday. Lived in Edmonton. It was walking distance.' He looks at me.

'Streatham,' I say. 'That's where I lived.'

'Oh, yeah,' he says – it could be Samarkand. 'With your Mum and Dad?'

'Well,' I say, 'there's the point.'

27

'Really?'

'You don't mind me being personal?'

'We goin' to get to you marrying the eleven-year-old, then, are we?'

'She wasn't eleven when I married her.'

'No offence, chum!'

'None taken.'

'So your Dad?'

'He came back for the weekends.'

'Hallo,' he says, 'here we go again.'

4

Banks throws the ball out to Moore who carries it up the left side of centre-field. But his pass to Hurst is snuffed out by Schnellinger, who puts the ball out of play. Hurst throws in to Ball who, seeming much alone, tries to take the ball to the goal-line. But Höttges and Schulz make an efficient triangle around him and draw the ball back to Tilkowski.

Tilkowski then punts the ball away extravagantly, but only out of play to the left. Jack Charlton takes the throw-in and finds Stiles, with space enough to range forward, but he loses control and the ball bounds back so that Cohen has to retrieve it. He draws it inside to Jack again, who pushes it forward to Peters in the centre circle. Running across field and slightly to his right, Peters seems to feel some urge to slant the ball back across his body to an inside-right position. That might have been a penetrating pass, but Moore, behind him and to the left, calls for it and Peters quietly lays it back, letting the set-up build, but opting out of being decisive.

Moore plays it on to Wilson, who lays it back to Moore who finds Stiles going over to the left. But again, Schulz and Höttges work their squeeze and return the ball safely to Tilkowski.

England put several tidy passes together there: they played possession football. But at a pace that let the defence get organized. That urge – a twitch almost – that Peters rejected, was a moment and a position where one of the really great players (a Law, a Puskas, a Pelé) might have cut through a scrambling defence with one stroke.

The Germans are moving on their left again. Schnellinger passes forward to Held, who lays it back and inside in the path of the advancing Beckenbauer. This is a key moment, if very brief. Beckenbauer has not been too active so far, and yet he is someone who could win the game for Germany (he has scored four goals in this World Cup so far; more than that, he is a maker of goals; in hindsight, we recognize that he was the most constructive player on the field that day). Now he is moving with the ball. Nobby Stiles, ten yards away, is briefly dancing with the referee as they try to avoid collision. Beckenbauer puts the ball one yard too many ahead of himself. Stiles darts out of the dance, like a thief, and makes the perfect tackle on the young German.

The event isn't much noticed, but it is brilliant for Stiles and surely it depresses Beckenbauer. For Stiles moves on and takes a return pass from Moore. He is too far out to shoot, but he tries anyway. There is a deflection and the Germans have possession again – but Beckenbauer had left space clear. It is a warning to him, and he is too young yet, too sensible, to ignore it. He begins to play defensively.

But the German attack that follows acquires weird threat. A rather aimless through ball comes to Jack Charlton who bends to head it down – right at the feet of Seeler. What's Jack got his long body for? Seeler sees a fresh opportunity and tries a long shot. Ray Wilson is on him and so the shot careens high and wide for a corner, its bounce too steep for Banks.

Haller takes the corner, a conventional inswinger, but there is no-one there to hinder Jack Charlton's strong clearing header. That falls to his brother Bobby, who pushes it forward to Hunt, who at last is moving towards goal. As Hurst comes up alongside him, Hunt lets Hurst serve as a decoy –

'Nice one, Roger,' says my friend.

– and lays the pass across field to Stiles, who clearly is not being properly marked. Stiles crosses and Hurst and Tilkowski are in contention for the ball. The German keeper makes a feeble punch away to the right, the opposite of commanding – this first time, he looks very shaky in the air. Bobby Charlton gathers it out on the left and lobs it back. Now Hurst really challenges Tilkowski in the air. There is contact: a shoulder in the keeper's face and Tilkowski is prostrate. The ball goes out to Ball on the edge of the box. He has a chance, but the referee says he has pushed Overath – when really, it seems as if the referee wants attention for the injured Tilkowski. In a few seconds, West Germany have looked horribly vulnerable.

From the free kick, Overath tries to set something up with Held and Seeler. But Jack Charlton takes it away. He gives it to Ball and then is supple and smart enough to sway back as the wall pass comes too high to him. He nods it down and moves on with rare control, and gives it left and forward to Peters. Then as Peters advances, so Jack begins to sprint forward out of some instinct. Peters carries on and puts in something that is not quite a shot and not quite a cross. Tilkowski 'saves' it, pushing it away for a corner, when he maybe should have left it alone. By which point Jack Charlton, advancing very fast, is at the edge of the box. But it seems that Peters never expected such initiative in the team's stopper.

Never forget: Jack Charlton is a hard man, the centre-half for Leeds United, sometimes a little crude in defence, sometimes rough, sometimes filthy. But he has vision and a mind that far exceeds his usual skills. For a moment, for England, there, he looks like John Charles.

Ball takes the corner, and there is Hurst at the corner of the penalty area, volleying a shot, high and wide and far beyond his abilities. You watch this English team and you do understand Alf Ramsey's credo: play to your abilities – and with it, the subtext, don't look for anything too extraordinary, too dazzling. For this can over-excite a team and make them lose their concentration.

'Few more crosses, I'd say,' says my friend, 'and their keeper's jelly. If we had Greaves there now, I'd tell him, just hang about, Jim, wait for the geezer to drop it. That goalie's a disgrace for a game like this.'

How often we've seen it, at the Bridge and White Hart Lane, as Greaves became a poacher in the penalty area, waiting on a mis-step or a hesitation. He was so small and yet he moved over the mud those four or five paces with such suddenness and balance. He never laboured. He never seemed to lose his poise in running. So he was there to meet the ball, striking it, without any need to control it first. The great Jimmy Greaves and his left foot had a way of 'tidying up' in the box that was lethal. It is so hard not to think that he should have been here. Ramsey is right, Greaves has lost a little speed after his jaundice – he's not as good as he was. But still he's in a different class from Hunt or Hurst – not knocking them, they know it. And the Germans know it: put Greaves in their box and he's got two men on him, which leaves someone else free. Pelé used to win games just by going on the field. It changed the way people played Brazil. And with this crowd, don't you think a couple of times, for three or four strides, seeing the goal, smelling it, that Jimmy wouldn't have been fast again? That man ached for goals. He was always horny for them. Just like Law and Best. Fucking killers, nothing like them.

'So anyway,' I say, 'my Dad.'

'Yeah? Right.'

'The day my mother went into the hospital to have me.'

'Yeah?'

'He left her.'

'You're kidding! But what about the games you played in the kitchen?'

'He came back.'

'Well, thank God!'

'At weekends.'

'You're havin' me on?'

'I'm not. Hope to die.'

'Where'd he go?'

'For years I didn't know. St Albans.'

'St Albans!'

'Other side of London.'

'And he came back at the weekends?'

'About two weekends out of three.'

'What did you think?'

'I thought it was normal.'

You see, it was 1941 when I was born. And I didn't need to think anything for a few years. By the time I was old enough to wonder, my mother said, it's the war. Your Dad's away doing war work. And he was, he worked for a company then that made radios, Philco, and the radios were going in aircraft and such. Of course, he didn't make the radios themselves. He was in management. But it was war work, and he didn't have to go to fight.

I wonder whether that's why he took the job, for he was only thirty-three in 1941, and I suppose he'd have been called up. Yet he wasn't afraid, not in an obvious way. You see, we had a cast-iron air-raid shelter in the house where we lived, and the ground floor where my Granny, his mother, lived, yes, my mother and I lived with her in Streatham. And when there were air raids, we all went down to sleep in the shelter, so if there'd been a bomb and the house came down we might have been dug out. There was food and water in the shelter, and I can remember lying there in the dark hearing noises in the sky. But my father, when he came home at the weekends, he wouldn't go in the shelter. He stayed in his bed upstairs – took his chances, my mother said.

'So he's off to work all week, and then comes home?'

'Right,' I say. 'My best friend, Bryan, across the street. His Dad was in the Army. He hardly ever saw him. My uncle, he was in a prisoner-of-war camp. I don't remember him at all until after the war. And there he was one day at the foot of the stairs, and he looks up and says, "I'm your Uncle Reg. I'm too weak to get up there." He'd been treated so badly in the camp.'

'This I can understand,' says my friend. 'My old man was in the Merchant Marine. He was away months on end. You accepted it.'

'Right.'

'But the war ended.'

'Right,' I say glumly.

'And your Dad still didn't come home?'

'Just weekends. And Christmas, and Easter, and August Bank, and Whit.'

'He was in St Albans?'

'Apparently.'

'On his own?'

'No, he had another woman there.'

'Your mother knew that?'

'She did.'

'And she didn't complain?'

'Not to me.'

'What was she doing then?'

'Well, she was looking after me and his mother, my Gran.'

'Looking after her?'

'She wasn't up to it herself.'

'While he was off with another woman?'

'That's how I understand it,' I tell him.

He looks out at the field, the slight mist of effort and cigarette smoke, that haze of soccer matches, and he says, 'I'll go to the top of our stairs!' Then he reflects.

'Why'd he leave the day your mother was going to have you then?'

'He didn't want a child.'

'So why'd he come back?'

And on that question I'll leave you hanging, because I've been hanging there for ever.

5

Tilkowski taps the goal-kick sideways to Schnellinger, gathers the return – there is no English cover to threaten this process – and punts the ball away fifty yards. In the attempt to control it, Wilson fouls and so a free kick is set up some thirty-five yards out in the inside-right channel. Beckenbauer will take it. There is an air of menace, but the set-piece is meek and gentle and something that Moore can easily head away to Bobby Charlton. A contrite Beckenbauer hurries back to cover Charlton who moves the ball forward to Alan Ball who then cuts inside, moving quickly, carrying the ball some thirty yards. He passes crossfield to Peters who takes a shot from twenty-five yards, a wide bouncing shot, a measure without any chance – unless football is suddenly to be decided by shots on goal. Yet again, there's a feeling in the English attack that it's honourable enough to try a shot, rather than seek the one penetrating pass that can disable the German rear defence.

So, again, Tilkowski has a goal-kick, but this time he lets Schnellinger mount the attack. His pass up the right wing comes to Seeler, but there is Wilson at the same instant knocking against the backs of the German's heels. It's another free kick, and Seeler takes this one himself swiftly, to Haller, who gives it back to Seeler who then swings the ball across field to Schnellinger, who forwards it to Held.

The English defence is sturdily aligned, so rather than explore the left wing, Held draws back and from forty yards out tries a very speculative cross to the far side of the English penalty area.

It is going deep: Wilson and Haller both back off to cover it. But Haller is unbalanced, and gives up the pursuit. Thus Wilson rises to the ball unchallenged; he has a few yards clear all around him. He will say later that he mistimes his jump, but this is not evident. Instead, he seems too intent on making an accurate downward pass with his header. He succeeds all too well.

The ball is tidily put down for the waiting Haller. It bounces. He wheels to his right. He controls it. It bounces again and the slight backspin from his stopping of it brings the ball back on to his right foot shot.

Moore lunges at this blow. In some reports it is said that he gives it a minor deflection. This is not apparent, as the ball moves across the goal between a stricken Jack Charlton and Banks's frantic, belated dive. England will say it is a soft goal, in that Banks and Jack momentarily thought the other one had it covered. But the shot is very accurate. It hits the stanchion in the far corner at the back of the goal. Give Haller credit: he has pounced on Wilson's mistake in an utterly professional way. Jack Charlton makes a bitter gesture with his arms, waving German glee and fate away. But there is no denying it: 0–1.

At home, I hurl Mathew's ball across the room: it bowls out the fire irons, and he looks at me in delicate alarm.

In Wembley's dense, dour throng, my friend turns to me in mockery that extends to self and any daft hope for glory in life. 'That's it,' he says – as immobile in the crowd, indeed as helplessly stuck, as Beckett's tramps, waiting for Godot – 'I'm off. I'm not hanging around for misery.'

Do you have to be English to know what he means? The greatest dread on this day we have been waiting for has been, quite simply, the plate of ashes we may have to eat. The unbearable thing about the big opportunity is the closeness of tragedy and loss. That's what makes you want to postpone the kick-off one day, and then another day. For there is something wretched in coming so far and then failing at the last step. It leaves you wondering whether you should have ever entered the Cup in the first place. I mean, finally, is even winning worth the risk of losing? Or are winners left haggard, haunted, and exhausted by the nightmare they saw in their sleep?

We are at the lowest essence of things here, and if I am not sure I understand the matter completely, still I know this is vital to being English.

In 1948, the Olympic Games were held in London, and the track events took place at this same Wembley arena. My father had been taking me to see athletics for a year or so, at the old White City arena. I was already a fast runner myself, and I was deeply fond of the sprinter E. MacDonald Bailey – a Trinidadian, but the English champion in those days. I had never seen a race, 100 yards or 220, that he didn't win.

My father and my mother took me to one day of the Olympic athletics – we saw Zatopek run, Mal Whitfield and Cochrane, the American hurdler. But it was the day of the 100 metres final, and we had seats on the straight where that race was run. MacDonald Bailey was in the final. There were three other black men in the race, so I was oddly unable to pick out Bailey. The starting gun fired and everyone in the crowd stood up. In ten seconds, it was more than anyone could do to hoist me up to *see* the thing. As the wall around me settled down, my father said, 'I think he was last.'

I wept hot tears. Last!

Someone named Harrison Dillard had won, from the USA – even then, I marvelled at a country that could come up with a sensational name like Harrison Dillard. Another American was second, Barney Ewell, and a third fifth, Mel Patton. Lloyd LaBeach of Panama was third –

'He's a kind of American, too, really,' said my mother.

McCorqurdale of England was fourth, and my Mac was sixth. Last! I burned with shame and disappointment.

'Well, he was in the final,' said my father.

I was beyond comfort.

So my father pointed out a large sign at one end of the stadium – the same stadium where we've just gone 0–1 down – where some words were printed. As near as I recall, it said that 'The important thing is not to have won but to have taken part.' This, it was explained to me, was the motto, the very watchword and ideal of the Olympic Games, and it had been said by a Frenchman, the Baron de Coubertin.

I could read the words for myself, even if every piece of story and folklore an English boy of seven had in those days taught him to mistrust French barons.

'So why did they race then?' I asked. 'Why do they run if winning doesn't matter?'

'It's just a game,' said my Dad. 'The winning shouldn't matter. After all, most people are going to lose, aren't they? And you can't have a race without the losers. You shouldn't run a race if you don't know how to be a good loser.'

I'm crying again as I'm writing this – I have to tell you. This is the mystery of life as far as I can see. Because I know my father was right, and I know he was wrong – and I know that July 30th 1966 means as much as it does to me, and to English football, I think, for good and ill, because of so great, and challenging, a win. You see, I am American now – officially, in my passport and my relationships with income tax authorities; I have sons who might be President. And America has a different view of this mystery: it believes in winning with a clear conscience. There are sayings on the wall in America like, 'Nice guys finish last', and 'Winning isn't the most important thing – it's the *only* thing!'

There were years in England, growing up with sports, when it seemed that one had to recognize the necessity, the duty almost, of English contenders to lose in the most important contests. We went to Wimbledon every year in the late 1940s and the early 1950s, on the first Saturday, when you could walk up, if you walked up early enough, and get good seats on Court Number 2. And year after year, men of a different strength and force from

Australia and America – Sedgeman, Savitt, Seixas, McGregor – would demolish the English champion Tony Mottram. My father would talk about how Fred Perry, an Englishman, had won Wimbledon three years in a row in the 1930s – and how Perry had then 'gone to America', if not just physically, why emotionally, because he preferred it. And no Englishman had won the Wimbledon title since – that was sixty years ago, but it is true still.

In boxing, it was proverbial that some game, brave, dumb Englishman was fighting an American for the title – and was going to come close to losing his life. Bruce Woodcock was the British heavyweight champion in the late '40s – a big man from Doncaster, until rather ordinary American fighters, Joe Baksi and Lee Savold, came to London and toppled him. Rocky Marciano mauled Don Cockell, in San Francisco, in 1955. Freddie Mills lost his cruiserweight world title to American Joey Maxim in London, in 1950.

There was one heady, short-lived exception to this. On July 10th 1951 – I was allowed to sit up in bed to listen on the radio – Sugar Ray Robinson came to London to fight the British middleweight champion, Randolph Turpin. Robinson was what the English called a 'swank', a 'big head', a show-off. He was also, my Dad admitted, maybe the best boxer in the world. It was hard for me to follow a fight on the radio. I couldn't tell who was winning. But I can recall the voice of the commentator, Raymond Glendenning, cracking at the end of the last round as the referee totted up his scorecard and then, 'Turpin! Turpin has won!' Throwing pillows; too thrilled to sleep. A good clean, close victory – and maybe Sugar Ray did take him too lightly in what had been meant as a European holiday. Two months later, at Madison Square Garden in New York, in the obligatory return, Robinson knocked the valiant Turpin out. Made it quite clear who was the better man. So that was that, and always was. Two months before the World Cup Final – in London, at Highbury Stadium, I think – Cassius Clay, as he then was, had cut the amiable, able Henry Cooper to pieces in six rounds – but only after 'Enry had caught the cocky Clay and put him down.

Henry Cooper was a terrific loser: generous, plucky, entirely and cheerfully Cockney, never a quarter of an inch arrogant or above himself. One of the most popular men in Britain at the time. Whereas Clay – it seemed obvious to British eyes – was a bit of a nutter, somewhere between crazy and a showman. Instead of one of those people who alter the world.

We always lost the Ryder Cup. The British Open at golf was invariably won by visitors – Bobby Locke, Bob Charles, Gary Player and then Palmer, Nicklaus and Watson. Roger Bannister broke the four-minute mile that night in Oxford (3 minutes, 59.4 seconds). I saw it a few months later on a screen in a shop that was demonstrating the new television sets – with Bannister collapsing like the dying swan at the end, though it wasn't a real race so much as a record attempt. In the real race, the Olympic 1,500 metres, Bannister came fourth. At the Oval, in 1948, Ray Lindwall bowled England out for 52. A couple of years later, 'with those little friends of mine, Ramadhin and Valentine', not to mention Worrell, Walcott and Weekes, the West Indies came as visitors and humiliated England.

One thing you could count on: an English team would win the Boat Race – unless Oxford sank.

And then here's this story. My Dad was a good tennis player. And as he came home at weekends, he joined a local tennis club, the Wigmore – eight hard courts behind Becmead Avenue, it's still there. One year, this would have been like 1954, he entered the annual summer competition at the club. Just put himself down as a spare man in the mixed doubles, and got drawn with a young American woman who was visiting for the summer. They played well together, and they advanced to the semi-final.

I went along to watch that game: indeed, I scored. I knew vaguely that the following weekend, the date for the final, was one when my father would be 'away'. But in the semi-final, a good, close game, he and the American girl were gradually winning. He *was* a good player: quick, deft, full of drop shots and slices, and not inclined to make mistakes. She was stronger than he was – along the lines of young Billie Jean Moffitt, aggressive, athletic, and grunting – I'd never heard that in a woman player before. And if a pretty woman grunted on the social tennis court in 1954 you knew she was serious.

'Our' side got to match point, when my father, who was serving, strolled to the net bouncing a ball on the red clay, and explained that since he couldn't be there next week for the final it was only fair to default now and let the other couple go ahead. The other couple were bewildered. The American girl stormed off the court, the healthy flush of exertion turning to rage. He'd never told her about the problem, or explained his theory of losing gracefully.

6

Kick-off. Peters circles with the ball briefly and then passes back to Jack Charlton, who gives it on to Stiles. He is tackled, but the ball bounces clear to Bobby Charlton, who moves left and sends it on to Hurst on the left wing. Hurst loops back and passes across field to Peters. But this ball is on line with the referee. Herr Dienst jumps to let it come through, and Peters seems a little startled by that and the abrupt arrival of Overath, who robs him. Overath then finds Haller, who draws the ball inside to Seeler. He gives it back to Overath, who passes to Haller and then, noticeably, falls back instead of running into space ahead of Haller down the right wing. Are Germany reckoning to guard their lead this early? A ball back to Overath in that clear pocket must have been dangerous. Instead, Haller draws the ball all the way across-field to Held, who puts in an early left foot cross. It is curling away, but Moore clears it.

Schnellinger, on the German left, passes the clearance inside where Beckenbauer, of his own momentum, heads it back to Schulz who, from way back in his own half, sends it to Haller on the right wing. He plays it off immediately, back to Beckenbauer, who is moving up the centre of the field. But he slips in the rich turf, and Peters moves in to pick up the ball.

Then, as earlier, Peters races upfield, carrying the ball – it is a stirring sight, but no one knows what he intends. And at thirty or so yards out, he tries another of those long shots. This one strikes Höttges and rebounds all the way to Cohen, who lifts a loose cross or pass forward but sailing over the heads of Hunt and Weber and out of play. Is Peters under instruction to shoot from any range, or is he an example of possession play that cannot always divine a final, decisive way of using the ball?

Tilkowski's goal-kick is cleared by Jack Charlton, but it only falls to Schnellinger, who gives it to Beckenbauer, who passes on to Haller. Though rather ponderously, Haller slips Stiles's tackle, which is enough to have Stiles snap back at him with a foul. Stiles is irritable about the whistle. Beckenbauer takes the free kick and passes to Haller, but then Beckenbauer declines to support attack and falls back on defence.

Haller loses the ball to Bobby Charlton, who seems very uncertain what to do. His long ball is headed in the direction of Hunt, but Weber (who seems as quick as the English forward) knocks it out of play. Schulz picks up the ball after the throw-in, but his long ball is deflected out of play again, so Höttges throws in and the ball is kicked away deep into the English half.

Moore gathers and he gives it by way of Jack Charlton to Cohen. As the full-back advances, Charlton moves outside him to the right to make an overlap. But Cohen passes on to Hunt, who gives to Peters, who is in turn beaten by Weber, who puts the ball out of play. The German tackling is toughening up now.

The ball goes in and out of touch a few times down the German left before Haller begins to work a little close interaction with Overath. This ends only when Emmerich misjudges a return wall pass to Overath, one that might have freed him. Ball makes off with the loose ball and Overath plainly trips him from behind. It is not a bad foul, but it seems to show a growing determination in the Germans to shut the game down.

The free kick goes leftward to Wilson, but his forward pass only slides out of play. The German throw-in goes to Tilkowski, who then throws left to Emmerich, whose pass to Haller is errant enough for Ball to take control. A touch to Peters gives it on to Bobby Charlton, but his pass goes out of play once more. England seem unable to develop their attacks.

Weber throws in to Tilkowski, whose big punt is headed out by Moore. It goes to Stiles, who quickly passes on to Bobby Charlton, who nicely swerves left and around Beckenbauer, beating him. Charlton passes sideways, left to the advancing Moore who stops in his tracks, reverses and draws a foul from Overath. Free kick.

Moore is reaching for the ball even as he scrambles to his feet. He steps back and makes to take the kick. But he hesitates a split second at what he sees, takes a two-step run and chips the ball forward thirty yards so that it drops like a hat on the twisting head of Hurst, who has run sideways into inexplicable space about seven yards from goal, but in front of goal. Hurst is adept at positioning himself for such headers, and his suppleness gives the ball more than enough force to pass a rooted, stranded Tilkowski. The ball bounces on the goal-line itself. 1–1, a gorgeous goal, maybe the smartest of the match and due in part to a certain West Ham rapport, but essentially to Moore's calm vision and priceless accuracy. There can be hours of inept labour sometimes on a soccer field, ordeals of goal-lessness, and then a goal so clean and simple it looks easy. Moore has found such a moment and found it at a time when England were plainly losing confidence.

Two goals so far, and you could argue that they were both the result of mistakes: Ray Wilson misplayed the cross and gave it to Haller on a plate; the German defence allowed Hurst to get into a sitter position without anyone marking him.

God knows, football is not abundant in goals – and over the years, they have been harder to come by all the time. Consider these figures for the decade that spans the 1966 World Cup. In a full season of 42 matches, these were the top-scoring teams for the following seasons:

1958–59	1959–60	1960–61
Wolves 110	Wolves 106	Spurs 115
Manchester United 103	Manchester United 102	Wolves 103
Arsenal 88	Spurs 86	Burnley 102

1966–67	1967–68	1968–69
Manchester United 84	Manchester United 89	Everton 77
West Ham 80	Manchester City 86	Chelsea 73
Leceister 78	West Ham 73	Leeds 66

Last season, 1994–95, the three top-scoring teams (still in a 42-match season) in the Carling Premier Division were:

Blackburn Rovers	80
Manchester United	77
Nottingham Forest	72

This year, 1995–96, as I write (December 5th), the top-of-the-table team, Newcastle, have 33 goals from 15 games. Chelsea, around the middle of the table, have played 16 games from which they assembled 21 points and 15 goals.* Chelsea have already played in four goal-less draws. I saw one of them, against Sheffield Wednesday, when not even the sophisticated Ruud Gullit could engineer a goal. He pulled a muscle late in the game and went off – but it could have been that he was just weary and depressed from having the Chelsea players give him the ball and stand around waiting for a miracle.

In the 1930–31 season, from 42 matches, Aston Villa scored 128 goals. Dixie Dean still holds the individual single-season record with 60 goals for Everton in 39 matches in 1927–28. In more recent decades, some of the great scoring records are:

George Best – 137 goals in 361 matches for Manchester United;

Geoff Hurst – 180 goals in 409 matches for West Ham; and

Jimmy Greaves who retired in 1971, aged only 31, with 357 goals scored at Chelsea, Spurs and West Ham.

* As of January 1st 1996, Chelsea had 25 goals in 24 games.

There's no-one playing now, I fear, who will approach the Greaves record – and no-one is ever going to threaten the highest scoring rate in all of English football history which belongs – in case you've been deaf – to one Brian Clough who, before injury ended his career, had scored 251 goals in 274 matches with Middlesbrough and Sunderland.

It's easy to think of explanations for the modern scarcity of goals: defenders have been transformed in the last fifty years – they have gone from being hard men, stalwart stoppers, to athletes. They are faster, more skilled, and there are more of them. Teams going on the defensive never settle for a goalie and five players. The penalty area has become increasingly crowded. There is man-to-man marking plus the extra zonal cover of sweepers. And goalkeepers are not just surer now; they are better protected by the rules. There was a Cup Final once, in 1958, when Nat Lofthouse of Bolton simply scored by barging Harry Gregg into the Manchester United goal as he held the ball!

So defenders are better – and singlemindedly offensive players have become a rarer breed. 'Forwards' are now expected to fall back in coverage; they have a midfield work rate to live up to. And it is seldom the fashion now for forwards, strikers, wingers, or whatever, to try to beat a man – to dribble the ball past them, to leave them on their backs, floundering. Many defenders won't even attempt the tackle; they back off, luring the aggressor into denser coverage.

And so we have seen a game develop in which it is often shrewd to wait upon mistakes in the defence. You play possession until some obvious gap, slip or error occurs. Or, as is still often the case in England, you boot the ball into the opponents' penalty area and wait to gobble up a flawed clearance. As the total of goals scored drops, it is more reasonable for managers to urge this approach. 'We steal one against them, and how are they going to beat us?'

To counter that, defensive players are taught greater skills and more theory. One consequence of this was the dire World Cup Semi-Finals of 1990 when the two matches – Argentina versus Italy and West Germany versus England – were 1–1 after extra time, and settled by a penalty-kick shoot-out. Disaster, depression, dead end. Penalty shoot-outs are an abomination. Teams should play on, sudden death, until, someone, anyone, scores a proper goal.

When kids go out to play football in the park or on the Common – as they do still, as I did for years – they pile their sweaters on the ground to make goal posts and they'll have a goalie and defender against two kids just trying to score goals. Six goals and you change round. There's no midfield build-up, no cover, no possession. You just home in all the time on the goal and the sight of the ball sliding beneath the goalie's dive and splitting the sweaters. That rush is as great as seeing a real net bulge with the orgasmic bullet and the great devouring roar of acclaim that bursts from the crowd in tiers behind the goal.

Scoring is passion, liberty and exercise. Boys wouldn't play without goals, and the big game needs to remember the sheer lust of professional basketball games, say, where you're scoring all the time, and at the end it's 128–127. That's a sport for exultation, whereas 0–0 needs Lithium or liquor. That's why Hungary needed to score 6 and 7 against England. That was the brutal satisfaction at the end of the 1962–63 season, when Chelsea got back into the First Division, when it had all depended upon the last game, at home, to Portsmouth.

It was an evening match, well into May. I remember after the game, talking to someone who took neither the game nor Chelsea that seriously. But there had been over 50,000 there, and you could feel the stir in south-west London.

'Did they do it, then?' she wondered.

'They did,' I grunted.

'Close, was it?'

'7–0,' I conceded, like a very well-fed man. And I still wouldn't mind one bit if this book could be called 5–2.

7

So Germany kick-off for the second time, and now both sides know that immaculateness has gone for the day. They can be a little more relaxed: the struggle slips from being virginal to marital. This is not an entirely fanciful comparison: in a game of few goals, equalizers permit a sudden maturity and even an elegant nonchalance instead of the striving to impress or take advantage.

Overath gathers the kick-off and sends it back to Beckenbauer, who tries a probing ground ball down the centre of the field. But it is beyond Seeler's reach, and Jack Charlton controls the loose ball and sends it forward to Ball. Thence it goes to Hurst and to Peters, moving forward purposefully. Wilson begins to make a bold overlapping run down the left. Peters sees it, but seems to judge that the pass – by necessity a chip over Hurst and at least one German – is too tricky. So he gives it back to Hurst, who in turn tries to deliver it to Wilson. But surprise is gone now, the ball is a step beyond Wilson and as it rolls towards the goal line the Germans retrieve it and pass it sideways to Tilkowski. At the same time there is a collision, perhaps accidental, between Ball and Schnellinger. Tilkowski still elects to punt the ball away and Moore easily heads it clear. Wilson tries to flick it on, but Schnellinger – working more to the right now, it seems – gathers it and passes out to Seeler, nearer the wing. Seeler comes across field with the ball and there is a comic collision with Schnellinger before Seeler resumes his dribble and lays it off, all too obviously, to Held. In turn, Held rejects the notion of going down the wing, cuts inside and tries a long shot. There is a deflection: Stiles easily takes the gentled ball away. He knocks it up to Jack Charlton, who settles for an old-fashioned boot-away. This drops over Weber's head, but he quickly recovers and passes to Höttges.

He gives to Overath, who plays it to Haller. His pass goes to Schnellinger, who slips an attempted tackle by Ball (is there a hint of grievance there?), and passes to Beckenbauer, who sends it out to Haller on the wing. This is a pretty build-up, but Haller's cross is without much interest, and Cohen easily clears it from in front of the left-hand goalpost. It may be too much to expect the reliable English full-backs to make the same mistake twice.

The clearance goes by way of Wilson to Moore, whose attempt to pass it up the left touchline goes out of play. From the German throw-in, Haller tries a clever flick inside, but there is no-one to exploit it. Ball wins control and gives it to Moore, whose touchline pass to Hurst is put out of play by a German. Hurst takes a quick throw-in and Ball begins to break inside, dribbling rapidly. To his right, Peters moves up fast but Ball is slow to see or make the pass, and by the time he strikes the ball it is not quite a shot, not quite a cross. The trained body will always kick a ball, just to be doing something, unless the mind tells it not yet.

Tilkowski rolls it clear to Schulz, who carries the ball over the half-way line, gives it to Haller (and then scuttles back to restore the German defence). Haller gives to Held, who tries one more big chip shot into the English goal area, a sad and automatic effort from someone who, earlier on, seemed to feel a chance in going outside defenders down the left wing. The chip is safely cleared by Jack Charlton. Schnellinger knocks it back, but too deep, and as Wilson and Seeler go for it, Seeler is rather fussily whistled for use of the elbows.

Out of the free kick, Banks punts away from the edge of his penalty area. Beckenbauer makes a very good headed clearance which falls to Peters, whose control is too measured to resist Overath's challenge. As Overath takes the ball away, Peters fouls him – and has his name and number taken. His West Ham manager, Ron Greenwood, has sometimes opined that Peters is a player years ahead of his time, but today he has looked a beat behind the ball, too cautious and too obvious.

Schnellinger takes this free kick, deep towards the far goal post, where Seeler rises clearly above Wilson to head the ball down. Banks makes the save tidily, but this is a sign of some genius left in Seeler still, notably the ability to out-jump bigger men. Banks punts clear again, towards the right, and a German mis-timed header sends the ball out of play. Cohen takes the throw from Charlton and gives it back to Bobby, who then slips Beckenbauer's tackle and moves across field, hinting at what might be a left-foot shot across his body. This is the famous Bobby Charlton in motion, but he finds himself running into the defence. He feeds it off to Ball, who is tackled forcefully, by Schnellinger again. The ball runs clear to the right and falls to the advancing left foot of George Cohen. A leg that is normally used for standing on then tries a remote shot that seems more threatening to Harrow than anywhere on Wembley's pitch.

During English attacks now, there is a section of the crowd that begins to sing, 'When the Saints Go Marching In', replacing 'Saints' with 'Reds'. It's half-hearted, and it's even a little clerical to have the unfamiliar 'Reds' added in. There's nothing yet like the full-throated roar of song that one knows from Old Trafford or Anfield. But, of course, there's not the emotion – not yet anyway – in supporting England that there is in club football.

But as you watch this Wembley first half, and hear the attempt at song, you cannot escape the rare sentimental appeal of Bobby Charlton and Manchester United. Maybe if England are to win today the load of their past has to be delivered.

Manchester United won the Cup in 1948 with what seemed a tremendous side: Crompton; Johnny Carey, Aston; Anderson, the splendidly named centre-half Allenby Chilton, Henry Cockburn;

Delaney, Morris, Rowley, Pearson, Mitten. Somehow I saw bits of that game on what would have been someone else's very early television set. And since I supported the other side, the Blackpool of Stanley Matthews, I felt crushed by the sheer power of United. Then three times in the 1950s – '51–52, '55–56 and '56–57 – United won the First Division title (by four points, eleven and six, respectively).

That third season, they were in the Cup Final, too, and thus within reach of the mythical 'double', something never yet managed. The team they fielded that day, against Aston Villa, at Wembley was:

Wood

Foulkes   Byrne

Coleman   J. Blanchflower   Edwards

Berry   Whelan   Taylor   B. Charlton   Pegg

They were known as the 'Busby Babes', because this was, essentially, a team recruited out of school by Matt Busby, the Scot who had managed United since the end of the war. This was his own team, very young, hand-picked and touched by majesty already. But they lost at Wembley that day, 2–1, because of the way the rules worked.

Six minutes into the game, Peter McParland, the electric and aggressive Villa winger, charged the United keeper, Ray Wood, who suffered a broken cheekbone. Today, he might have been sent off for assault. Then, Wood was carried off and could not be replaced. Jackie Blanchflower went in goal and United had to play 84 minutes with ten men. Even then, they nearly equalized at the end.

So the 'double' was denied. The next year, 1957–58, United, as League champions, were in the European Cup, for the second year running. They had entered the previous year despite the incredible, inane and ghastly refusal of my blessed Chelsea to risk the competition in the season after their lone League championship, 1954–55.

In early 1958, United were duly progressing in the European Cup. On February 4th they played the second leg of the quarter-final match with Red Star Belgrade, away. At Old Trafford, United had won 2–1; in Belgrade, they managed a 3–3 draw in front of a hostile Yugoslav crowd. So they were through to the semi-final.

Their plane home, an Elizabethan of British European Airways, landed to refuel at Munich. It was snowing. There was slush on the runways. The plane prepared to take off, but then braked. Something was wrong. The pilot tried again, without success. He then asked the passengers to return to the departure lounge. But after ten minutes there, they were called back. They got in the plane: it was 2:55 p.m.

The Elizabethan accelerated down the runway once more. It just cleared the ground, hit a fence and then a house and broke up. Bobby Charlton came to spilled out of the aircraft, lying in the snow. Dennis Viollet, next to him, was bleeding. Matt Busby, a few yards away, couldn't move. Harry Gregg, the goalie, was trying to help. The report came in on the radio for the 6:00 news, and I think it was the worst I had ever heard. When it was all said and done, three Club officials (including the coach, Bert Whalley) were dead, eight journalists (including the fine England goalkeeper, Frank Swift who, my Dad said, could pick up the ball in one hand) were dead, and of the playing staff, the dead were:

Roger Byrne: left-back for England, 19 caps already
Geoff Bent
Eddie Coleman: as everyone anticipated, a future England player
Duncan Edwards: 10 England caps already, and a fearsomely great player

Mark Jones
David Pegg: left-winger, 1 England cap so far
Tommy Taylor: centre-forward, 13 England caps already
Bill Whelan: a brilliant Irish inside-forward.

United did not miss a game. Matt Busby, who was badly injured, was in hospital for some time. Jimmy Murphy took over the team for the interim. They bought a couple of new players; other Babes were brought on fast; and people like Bobby Charlton, Harry Gregg, Bill Foulkes, and Dennis Viollet – all on the plane – got on with it. That year, 1957–58, the terrible year, United did a strange double; they were still second in Division One, to Wolves; and they lost the Cup Final to Bolton. They were beaten in the semi-final of the European Cup, too, by Milan. To which city, of course, they flew for the match.

All of which is crucial to what happened that July Saturday in 1966. For English soccer found its heart in the Munich disaster. I am not certain how and when 'When the Saints Go Marching In' began to be sung at football matches, but I believe it began when the shattered United took to the field again. Generations have passed, but the feeling has never deserted Old Trafford. For most people of that time, whether they support Chelsea, Villa or Scunthorpe, they support Man United, too. Because of what happened, and of what it meant when Busby rebuilt the team and made it even greater.

You have to realize that, in all likelihood, the England team at Wembley in our game could have been:

Banks

Cohen   J. Charlton   Moore   Wilson

Stiles   Edwards   Ball

Greaves   Taylor   B. Charlton

Which is some team, though it lacks all our goal scorers.

You have also to add that, by 1966, United were:

Stepney

Cantwell   Foulkes   Brennan   Dunne

Crerand   Stiles   B. Charlton

Best   Herd   Law

They won the League in 1966–67.

You should understand how the eternally sad-faced Bobby Charlton is an emblem of that history, and how despite his magnificence, over the years he has always seemed touched by shyness, melancholy and a generosity to others so that he never wished to dominate. Or maybe that was just having Jack as a big brother.

This history leads to a mystery. For in its first issue in 1995, a new magazine, *Total Sport*, polled over a thousand sports writers and broadcasters to find 'their ten greatest British sports heroes'. Prowess was not the only criterion. Voters were asked to assess impact on the sport and on the public in general. Qualities of heroism were specially in order.

George Best was number 1. Ian Botham, 2; Linford Christie, 3; Bobby Moore, 4. Sir Bobby Charlton was 25. Stanley Matthews was 21. Brian Clough was 10. Greaves was 28. Bill Shankly was 31. Jock Stein was 34. Denis Law was 53. And so on. A fisherman was 98.

But nowhere in the top 100, apparently, was there room for the man who created, sustained and inspired the greatest of English club teams, Matt Busby.

'Diabolical,' says my friend, 'and there was no bloody Alf Ramsey, neither.'

8

As Tilkowski takes the goal-kick, a full, warm sun comes out, reminding one of May-time Cup Final days at Wembley with all of summer stretching ahead. The kick is flicked on by the deft Seeler who then picks up a half-hearted intrusion from Stiles and knocks the ball on for Haller who, outside the box, is demonstrably off-side. The first such call of the day.

From the free kick, Wilson's downfield ball is easily gathered by Schulz, who gives it to Schnellinger. There's a nice cross-passing build-up involving Seeler, Haller and Overath before the last player sends an aimless ball down the middle of the field to Banks. The greatest pressure in this kind of match, granted the highest levels of speed and fitness required, is to be sure that everything one does is purposeful and intelligent. No wonder if some players are content to pass the ball away, just to avoid a blunder.

The English clearance goes from Banks to Moore to Peters to Stiles, who is then tackled by Held. The ball goes to Haller now, who loops around in a crossfield run, feeds Emmerich who then lays it back to Held, who tries another big cross to the far post. Once more, Seeler out-leaps his cover, though it is Moore and Wilson, this time, but his header goes down and wide. This is Seeler's third World Cup, and he is in many ways the German counterpart to Bobby Charlton – a national hero, a wise, experienced man, but a kid whenever he feels the chance of running fast at goal. Still, Seeler's ability to win the ball in the air *is* recognized: as well as Moore and Wilson, we have Banks, Cohen and Stiles in the area of the goal-line. It is a way of appreciating that many players in the game take it for granted that their territory is the full length of this holding, sapping ground. Continuous soccer is a mighty test of stamina, and Ramsey has prepared for this.

Banks gives the goal-kick to Wilson, picks up the return and punts away towards Hurst, who is fouled on the left wing by Höttges. Wilson gives the free kick to Stiles, who relays it to Ball, who dances sideways, making Schnellinger strain to keep up. In turn, he passes to Bobby Charlton who is only loosely marked by Beckenbauer and so, on a side-long run, is able to put in a left-foot shot that draws a rather awkward full-length save from Tilkowski. These Charlton moments seem to deserve the sunshine that picks up his straw hair and the dome of his head.

Schnellinger clears the ball away. Yet again, Seeler rises above Moore to head it on. But there's no-one to use it except for Wilson, who draws the ball across field to Cohen. His pass is flicked on by Hurst and Tilkowski gathers the ball with Hunt in menacing, though rather theatrical, proximity. For most of the first half, Hunt has seemed out of his element, though eager to play a part.

Then something wondrous happens. The clearance goes to Beckenbauer. His forward pass reaches Seeler, who beats Moore with a feint one way and a whipping turn in the other direction. In the same movement, he gives the ball on to Haller – with Beckenbauer rushing forward in support. It is the sweetest move of the match, and Haller is clear, despite Wilson's closeness. There is every likelihood of a goal, but Banks has so foreseen everything that he is out at the edge of the penalty area to scoop the ball off Haller's toe. What is most impressive about Banks's save is that he makes it seem obvious. But many goalkeepers would have been stranded, seeing the need a fraction late and advancing with less than authority. Tilkowski, you feel sure, would have been lost.

'Flipping heck,' says my friend. 'These Germans are still good.'

'Beckenbauer and Seeler,' I say, 'they could win the match.'

'Don't lose heart.'

'I'm happy,' I shout back. 'I loved that move.'

'Our lads, they want to just calm it down a bit.'

But England can't be heartened when Bobby Charlton's notional upfield ball is matter-of-factly consumed by Schulz. Here come the Germans again: they're finding belief. Schulz gives it out to Emmerich, who lays it back to Seeler and moves on. The ball comes back to Emmerich, who hurtles forward, loses the ball to Jack Charlton's crisp tackle and then tumbles over Jack's thigh. The referee blows for a foul – a nonsense: Emmerich is nowhere near good enough a player to have had control of the ball or himself, and Charlton's contact was perfectly timed. It's an odd thing, for Jack Charlton can be a very skilled player yet, at Leeds above all, he has earned the wariness of referees.

Schnellinger takes the free kick, and England are at odds. Three times they attempt clearances before at last Peters tidies up. He gives it to Hunt and an attack builds, by way of Hurst, Moore and Ball, but finally Hunt is easily tackled by Weber from the side, the ball going into touch. Moore takes the throw-in to Ball, whose cross comes to nothing when Hurst is called for pushing Schulz.

Tilkowski punts away. Moore clears, and Ball plays it on. But possession goes to Germany, and then back to England again. There's another English attack, by way of Moore, Bobby Charlton and Cohen, but yet again Hunt is beaten at the close by Weber, conceding a corner. Ball takes it and seemingly proves his deadball accuracy by dropping it in Tilkowski's arms.

His clearance goes to Emmerich and on to Beckenbauer, but his pass to Seeler goes astray. Peters begins an attack. He gives to Ball who feeds Hurst. Bobby Charlton picks it up and gives to Stiles, who lays it away to Cohen. Then Cohen passes across field to the advancing Moore, whose long shot is still rising as it passes eight feet above the goal.

'Bobby!' my friend groans. 'What you doin', my son? We're not playing bloody rugby.' He turns to me, fellow-sufferer – we are companions in anxiety and dismay, and in both of us there is that London voice in which you can hear a twinge of sigh or whine in even chance remarks. 'Alf has to settle them down. Play for half time. Give 'em a talkin'-to.'

But Ramsey and the coaching staff are twenty yards from the sideline, sitting on their bench, and never picked on by the television cameras. Not that Alf would give much away if he came under scrutiny. He is not exactly avid for photo-opportunities.

I have been hard on Ramsey already, for embodying and bringing respectability to the notion that a Jimmy Greaves could be dispensed with. There were others who would be harder: Denis Law, for instance, predicted that the England method successful in 1966 would surely stifle the natural excitement of the game. By the 1980s, there were plenty of reasons for heeding that argument. And Ramsey was never truly liked by the public or the nation. Was he too shy or guarded for that? Was he always the victim of his own corporal-like starch? He could sound like a prig and a phony. Yet Alf Ramsey was a revolutionary, too, an inspired man (if seldom quite inspiring) and a life-long student of the game. That he often seemed, and made others feel, uncomfortable, only helps explain his complexity as a man.

So dark, so swarthy even, so awkward in small talk, he reminds me a little of Richard Nixon – a man who was so tormented that no-one seemed to like or trust him. Then there is the Malvolio in Ramsey, the Dagenham born-and-bred lad who wanted to rise above that lowly world. There's the grisly occasion when, asked about his parents, in an interview, whether they were alive still and where they lived, said, 'In Dagenham, I believe.' Of course, he knew where they were. He was fond and kept in touch. But he was ashamed of Dagenham, and he tried to make a little joke about it. Instead, it left him seeming cold and a stranger in his own life. It probably only happened because he had worked as hard to talk properly as he had to kick with both feet. He longed to escape lowliness; I'm sure there was a fire burning for glory in the man. But then he banked that fire down, smothered it in coal dust. He never knew how to show glory, never knew how to look like Denis Law, a living flame!

There are Ramsey jokes, of course: how he took two years off his age – because his playing career was delayed by the war; how he tried to avoid tackling as a full-back, in an age when full-backs were meant to be crunchers, because he often fell over and felt embarrassed getting up; and how, in the press conferences that fell to an England manager, elocution lessons would sometimes let him down so that he wandered into cul-de-sacs of obscurity. People treasured Ramsey-isms: he was a comic character, yet humourless – someone you laughed at. And he was physically rather squat, just as his face seldom took on a natural smile. Alf Ramsey could seem so composed you guessed at constipation. Added to which, he could damn himself with sudden, chilly glimpses of arrogance.

Yet he changed everything. After Army service, he signed up for Southampton, a Division Two team, for eight pounds a week. That was 1946; he was twenty-six. He worked very hard to make up for being slowish and a poor tackler. His positioning became remarkable. And no-one learns that without being able to read a game. As a full-back he was famous for his creative passes out of defence. People began to call him 'The General'. In the spring of 1949, he was signed by Arthur Rowe for Spurs. Nearly thirty, he still lived with his parents.

Shortly thereafter, he began to play for England. As so often in those days, a player was recognized if his club did well. In 1949–50, Spurs won the Second Division (by 9 points). The very next year, they won the First Division. Rowe's team played push-and-run, as it was known then – in other words, short passes and running off the ball to find a position worthy of being passed to. It was one of the most cohesive teams:

Ditchburn

Ramsey   Willis

Nicholson   Clarke   Burgess

Walters Bennett Duquemin Bailey Medley

'Know what Alf did?' says my friend. 'He got Ted Ditchburn to throw the ball out to him, instead of just belting it up-field. Keepers had never done that before. So Alf would build the attack from his own goal now. You should have seen him and Bill Nich together! Alf was . . . well, he was respected, know what I mean?'

But not loved. Best full-back in the country in those early '50s, but not a hero. Maybe he wondered why, and the more he wondered the grimmer he looked. Until you thought he was hiding something.

'Another life up in St Albans?' whispers my friend with a grin.

No, not that. But there was something hidden in Alf, something he couldn't show. Put it this way, Alf was someone Alfred Hitchcock would have liked. And that Alfred, also a touch too elocutionary for comfort, was born in Leytonstone, which is only a few pitches-length away from Dagenham.

9

Tilkowski's goal-kick launches an elaborate German build-up. Emmerich receives the kick out on the left. He feeds Overath, who lays it back to Schnellinger. The blond back seems readier now to press forward. He gives it to Overath, who pushes it out to Weber on the right – another defender moving up. The ball goes to Seeler and back to Weber again, and then to Haller and to Overath. This is all tidy, but not very progressive, and Overath's next pass across-field is too rapid for Schnellinger to gather. Ball and Held tussle for the loose ball, and the referee calls a foul on Ball, which prompts bitterness from the red-head more passionate than anything in the prior German build-up.

Schnellinger's free kick, lofted into the goalmouth, is no problem for Wilson. He clears to Moore, who sends the ball on to Hurst. But his pass forward to Peters manages to hit him mid-stride – Peters lacks nimbleness or the ability to adjust his steps quickly to take in a ball.

The new German move stems from Beckenbauer, who gives it on to Held. Whereupon, the German forward is nicely edged by one Charlton, Bobby, into the decisive tackle of the other, Jack. (Kids who played together in the streets of Ashington, Northumberland, with soccer thick in the family – Jack Milburn of Newcastle was their mother's cousin.)

Jack clears to Ball (who has Beckenbauer in attendance), who feeds to Stiles – yet again, Stiles has room for a training run. The ball then goes to Hunt, to Ball and back to Stiles, whose centre is put out of play by Schulz. Actually, it goes dead off Stiles, but the referee never sees this. So England steal a throw-in, but it quickly goes out of play again.

Schnellinger sends the new throw directly to Tilkowski, who hurls it down the left to Held. Beckenbauer and Weber carry it on around midfield, and Beckenbauer then sends the ball right to Overath, who passes to Schnellinger. His cross is headed on by Emmerich, but Seeler is beaten by Moore, who clears, by way of Peters, to Ball. But his pass forward to Hurst is snuffed out by Höttges, whose vigorous tackle sends the ball deep into the left of the English defence.

Wilson retrieves it, and works it up the left with Moore. It goes to Hunt, to Stiles, to Bobby Charlton, who then changes direction by swinging across-field to Cohen. Cohen then puts in a deep crossing ball to the area of the penalty spot where an advancing Hurst rises above Höttges and Weber (both tottering back) to send a dangerous header low to Tilkowski's right. The keeper goes down but he can only scramble it away to the right. Ball takes it away from Tilkowski's second dive, and tries a whirling pass back across the goal to Hurst, whose leap has carried him clear. But he is not quite quick enough, and a rapidly arriving Emmerich boots the ball out of touch. Tilkowski's saves manage to be as undermining as England's thrusts. The throw-in goes to Bobby Charlton. He feeds Moore, whose low drive is headed away by Seeler.

Emmerich picks up the clearance and gives it inside to Haller. He passes back to Held, who pushes a long ball forward for Emmerich to run on to. In fact, the pace of that pass is too much for Emmerich – the ball rolls harmlessly over the English goal line – but the thought was so penetrating it amounts to a score. On Wembley's big pitch, after thirty minutes of play, tiredness is beginning to join with enterprise, opening up gaps. The continuous flow of top-class soccer exerts a mounting pressure.

Banks clears away to Moore. He finds Stiles, who releases Peters in space. Peters sees the chance for a fast wall-pass exchange with Bobby Charlton, but Bobby's return is not accurate enough. Weber and Hurst contest the loose ball, which bounces clear to Peters, who sends in a chip shot to Tilkowski at his near post. The keeper gathers it safely, but one can see the point in testing him at every opportunity.

He punts the ball clear, deep into the English half. Seeler makes to challenge Moore for it, but Moore is now at his best. On one knee, stretching forward, he half-traps the ball. As it bounces up, he is there to take it on his chest before moving off to the left under control. A rattle of applause goes round the ground at this authority. The move forward comes to nothing when Höttges puts the ball into touch. But then, from the throw-in, Cohen's cross is cleared out to the left wing where Bobby Charlton retrieves it. He makes a return cross, not especially dangerous, and Tilkowski is seriously embarrassed in clearing it. The punch away is feeble; the attitude of his body is clearly intimidated.

But then, as English fans lick their lips, the Germans mount a disarming attack. Beckenbauer and Haller together bring the ball downfield before Beckenbauer releases Held on the left wing. It has always seemed possible that Held could trouble Cohen, and now that contest is on. But Cohen holds off, and Stiles is able to make a good tackle on Held. Then the English keep the ball close, in that corner. Stiles gives to Ball, who plays it back to Cohen. Held then challenges Cohen, who falters, recovers, circles and finally is beaten again by Held, who goes to the by-line where only Jack Charlton's swooping intrusion settles things.

Held takes the corner, with his right foot. Moore makes an incomplete clearance which falls to Overath at the eighteen-yard line. His snap shot draws a fine, instinctive blocking save from Banks when a goal was just as likely. The ball bounces away to Emmerich, who has a good shot from very close range, but one that Banks, nearly on his knees still, narrowing the angle, smothers perfectly. And holds. Two remarkable saves in a matter of seconds, done so fast they draw no attention to themselves. Banks is the best goalkeeper in the world, not least because he makes his saves discreetly and tidily. He must be the apple of Ramsey's eye. It will be four years before – in Mexico, against Brazil – Banks makes a save from Pelé, at such an extreme of hopelessness, that everyone has to see he is without equal.

We left Alf Ramsey with the great Spurs team. We have seen already that he lasted for England until that crucial defeat by Hungary in 1953. Two years later, the thirty-five-year-old was having trouble holding his place in the Spurs side. He was plainly slow by then, and he did not wait to be made a fool of. He retired as a player and immediately took the manager's job at Ipswich Town.

Ipswich then were in the Third Division South, a small, settled side in a town that lived contentedly enough on the cold shoulder of England. There was no money to throw around at the club, and no special ambition beyond having a team. Ramsey was out of the public eye and asked to do the best he could with a band of regular players – no stars, no one of unusual ability. It was a situation made for his stress on coaching, fitness and playing within your means. But in his first season there, Ipswich were promoted to Division Two. For a few years, they seemed to have found a natural level, finishing around the middle of the table. In 1959–60, they were eleventh, with 19 wins, 17 losses and 78 goals scored. But next year, they won that division and scored 100 goals – 40 for Ray Crawford and 30 for Ted Phillips. Those two strikers, workmen, not celebrities, were much aided by the winger Jimmy Leadbetter, who would play well behind them, laying on goals. Some even sniffed a bit of a 4–2–4 line-up in Alf's mind.

People were happy for the unpretentious Ipswich and the solid, thoughtful effort of manager Alf. But then, the very next year, 1961–62, in a Division One that included the Burnley of Jimmy Adamson, Ray Pointer and the immaculate Jimmy McIlroy, not to mention a Spurs team that had done the double the year before and which seemed invincible on paper:

<pre>
                        Brown
          Baker   Henry
    D. Blanchflower   Norman   MacKay
  Medwin   White   Smith   Greaves   Jones
</pre>

Ipswich won the championship! (To make that season more bizarre or ominous, Chelsea were also relegated to Division Two.) Crawford got another 33 goals, and Phillips got 28: and the Portman Road ground where Ipswich played had an average crowd of just over 22,500. It was both humdrum and miraculous, which I suspect was exactly how Ramsey liked things.

And that summer, after Ipswich's glory, the World Cup was played in Chile. The English manager was still Walter Winterbottom: he had been in the job since 1946. He was a devoted coach, a big talker, an eloquent analyst and a weak man, who had always accepted that he made selection recommendations that a committee then approved or altered. He was not in charge; and he never stood up and said that situation was daft.

England qualified for Chile, just as they had been to Switzerland in 1954 and Sweden in 1958. In 1954, they'd made it to the quarter-finals where Uruguay thrashed them. The Final that year was a surprise, for West Germany beat Hungary, 3–2. This was the Hungarian team that had trounced England, and which had itself smashed Germany 8–3 in an earlier round. But Puskas was hurt – he played anyway, to no avail. Germany proved hard and solid in a downpour, and brilliance was not enough.

In 1958, a year in which England, Northern Ireland, Scotland and Wales all qualified, England held Brazil to a goal-less draw but failed to make the quarter-finals. Incidentally, if you wanted to believe in *Britain*, their team that year could have been (even months after the Munich disaster):

Kelsey

Howe   Caldow

D. Blanchflower   Wright   MacKay

Douglas   McIlroy   J. Charles   Haynes   McParland

That's not a bad side – yet could it have beaten the Brazilians who triumphed over the host nation, Sweden, 5–2 in the Final?

Gilmar

D. Santos   N. Santos

Zito   Bellini   Orlando

Garrincha   Didi   Vava   Pelé   Zagalo

Brazil won again, of course, in 1962 in Chile, with much the same side. Along the way, they beat England 3–1 in the quarter-finals, a fine side and one that some of the players felt was the best England had ever had:

Springett

Armfield   Wilson

Moore   Norman   Flowers

Douglas   Greaves   Hitchens   Haynes   Charlton

But, counting Brazil in 1950, that was four World Cups in a row where Walter Winterbottom and England, the founders of the game, after all, had failed. A change had to come. Winterbottom resigned. The job was offered to Jimmy Adamson, the Burnley wing-half. He turned it down. Ramsey was next in line. He said, of course, gentlemen, and very soon thereafter he started announcing that England would win in 1966. Of course.

10

Having made the two saves, the always lugubrious-looking Banks gets up with the ball and throws it out, accurately. It reaches Bobby Charlton, who gives it back to Wilson, and then takes the return in midfield space. As always Beckenbauer is with him, but three steps away, covering without impeding. Bobby comes to a halt; he makes a gesture of kicking. But Beckenbauer will not be lured into trying a rash tackle. All the same, Bobby is winning their battle, and keeping Beckenbauer away from the attack. It's almost as if the young German has elected to study Charlton – it's a lesson that will bear fruit in future years. So Charlton sideways the ball to Stiles, who gives it to Cohen. Then Cohen's forward pass, into spaces Hunt wants to occupy, comes to nothing as Hunt is called for pushing.

From the free kick, Tilkowski throws to Haller, and the ball goes from Höttges to Beckenbauer – to Höttges to Beckenbauer. It is notable, and it must be a worry to Beckenbauer, that whenever the Germans have the ball going forward, Stiles attends him as if to say Charlton is behind him, waiting for error. Beckenbauer gives the ball meekly to Schnellinger, who moves it left, to Overath and Held, before Held's cross to the far post forces Wilson, modestly challenged by Haller, to head away for a corner.

Haller's corner kick, another in-swinger, is punched away by Banks and then traded backwards by Germany by way of Schnellinger and Weber to Schulz. He passes upfield to

Beckenbauer, but that is cleared by Jack Charlton. Again, the Germans put together a movement with Weber and Overath, but Schnellinger's through pass is far too strong, and allowed to cross the English goal-line.

England next, and then Germany, make brief, inept forays before Moore makes a tremendous effort to keep the ball from going out of play on the left. He rarely employs such speed, but he saves this ball and moves it up the wing to Hunt, who is, as it were, routinely dispossessed by Weber, who returns the ball to Schulz and Tilkowski.

The Germans come back with Seeler involving Overath and Beckenbauer, then Haller and Overath again, before Stiles makes the tackle. Then Moore sets up a further English attack, giving the ball to Peters, taking the return, and passing it on to Hurst. But as Hurst moves to play it off, the ball bounces back more forcefully than expected and into the path of Emmerich, who beats a Jack Charlton committed to support the attack. Emmerich is clear, if far out. England are exposed, and are only saved by Moore's desperate covering tackle. He is plainly strained by having to move at top speed twice in a short span, yet he sets up an attack, passing to Bobby Charlton. He gives it to Ball, whose pass to Cohen is a little behind the back and so ends up out of play.

Ball's throw-in goes to Cohen, whose low cross is headed clear by a diving Höttges. But Wilson gathers it, and whether by accident or design, lobs forward a pass that clears Weber and sets Hunt free and clear just to the left of the goal at the corner of the goal area. The ball is on Hunt's left. His angle is not wide. But one has to smell a goal, and picture Greaves's ruthlessness in such a position. Then Hunt shoots upwards and Tilkowski knocks the ball away.

The Germans come again with Seeler and Overath, but their efforts seem limp now. England seize the ball: Peters gives it to Bobby Charlton, who once more has Beckenbauer as a rather hypnotised shadow. Bobby carries Beckenbauer across-field and then slips a through pass in the reverse direction that runs beautifully for Peters. This may be a better chance than Hunt's, for Peters has a better angle and more room. But he is not lethally quick in the crisis, and Weber is able to kick the ball clear.

England could have had two more goals, and somehow Germany needs to reassert itself. Seeler receives the ball from Held, and then moves forward to the right of the England goal for 30 or so unchallenged yards. England are there in cover, but Seeler has had time to get balanced, and his long shot towards the top corner of the goal compels a diving Banks to tip the ball away for a corner.

Play is scrappy now – the players are waiting for half-time. England has one attack where Cohen gives Hunt the chance to move across-field with the ball. But yet again Weber blocks the Hunt shot. Germany wins another corner, but Haller's effort goes high and wide. And so it comes to pass that, as Ball is making his way forward on the right, Herr Dienst gives three long blasts on his whistle. Half-time.

England might easily be in the lead. Germany, on the other hand, have reason to feel fortunate about being on terms. The players make the long way back to the dressing-rooms. The crowd does whatever it can in the circumstances to stretch its legs. Half-time at soccer is too short a break for refreshments. English grounds, even today, offer the most miserable fare. But half-time is respite, and the game is on now, so tested, and the players so exercised, that no-one can be nervous any longer. Half-time, though, is the occasion when team managers are supposed to offer a few words of magic and insight.

Ramsey this day was calm, and orderly, and reliably matter-of-fact. 'You're doing very well,' he said. 'But you can improve. And if you do, you'll win.' He gave this word out, like a communiqué, flat and unemotional, yet quite certain. It is as if Ramsey prefers not to stoop to the inspirational – as if he knows his method, indeed his character, is sounder than that.

But he is right. The nation dismantled, humiliated or at best unlucky in four previous World Cups is within sight of a famous, business-like victory. In another forty-five minutes, say, this disconcertingly solemn and unimpassioned Ramsey could be proved right. And all along, for three years, he has looked to the team chosen to confirm that bald, breathtaking prediction: 'I say it again: I think England will win the World Cup in 1966. We have the ability, strength, character and, perhaps above all, players with the right temperament. Such thoughts must be put to the public, and particularly to the players, so that confidence can be built up.' This is the first time, in such a setting, that confidence has been spoken of like a muscle, bound to enlarge and improve with exercise.

There were those who laughed in anticipation at seeing Ramsey's dark pride vanquished by defeat in 1966. For he never made those predictions with a cheeky grin, or with any concession to all the fates being tempted. Of course, he was also, whether he intended this or not, taking some load off the players. They had something to live up to now, a very obvious target, but they were not quite the prime target for abuse if ever they played badly.

Alf Ramsey had established the particular role of the England team manager, and he had done so by quietly obliging his bosses, the Football Association, to change their ways, and to replace them with his system. He simply would not tolerate the notion that his predecessor, Walter Winterbottom, had not had the sole power to pick the players. He indicated that Winterbottom's reticence, albeit the mark of a gentleman, was proof of amateurism. Winterbottom had been to college and earned a teacher's diploma. He had been a school teacher, and he had had only a minor career as a player, spoiled by injury. He had never managed in the Football League, arguably the toughest competition in the world.

Ramsey was a star player, and a phenomenally successful manager. The FA could only have him for England on his own terms – absolute power and the minimum of interference. He wanted to be a professional manager, a full-time job, with a modest office at the Lancaster Gate offices of the FA. He was not much concerned about the money. He was encouraged to be bold by the parlous international record of England, especially when it travelled overseas. Many voices on the soccer scene had been calling for better leadership, greater skills of ball control, and more stress on individual genius.

Now, the Ipswich Town of Ramsey's glory was *not* that kind of footballing enterprise. Though Ray Crawford won a few England caps on the strength of his League goals, no-one supposed he had the class needed. Ramsey the player had been a model of living within one's limitations, and acting in a way so as to conceal them. He had been deeply influenced by Arthur Rowe's method at Spurs, and so one might have predicted his credo: don't make mistakes; pass the ball when you can't go forward; learn to pass accurately; run forever; and wait for goals.

More than that, Ramsey was a player's manager at a moment when the players had found new life and status. A soccer player in the 1930s, 1940s and 1950s might be a national hero before enormous crowds – and someone who was making a fair living and trying not to worry about what would happen to him when he got hurt, when he slowed, or was simply too old to keep his place. Players belonged to their clubs, who paid them (this by the late 1950s) £20 a week during the season and £17 in the summer.

Twenty pounds a week in 1960, say, was not a poor wage – I began work in 1961 as a copy-editor at a publishing house at £8 a week. But £20 nowhere near addressed the celebrity, the talent or the pressure on a football player. And when their clubs chose to sell them, to transfer them (like pieces in a board game), the sums were minor compared to those common now. Moreover, in those days, the players themselves got hardly any of the transfer fee. You can trace the progress made in the 1950s:

1951 Jackie Sewell from Notts County to Sheffield Wednesday for £34,000;

1954 Danny Blanchflower from Aston Villa to Spurs for £30,000;

1958 Albert Quixall from Sheffield Wednesday to Manchester United for £45,000;

1960 Denis Law from Huddersfield to Manchester City for £55,000.

In the early 1960s a test case was fought by George Eastham, the fragile but very cultivated Newcastle inside-forward. He wanted to leave Newcastle and get a better deal elsewhere. His contract was up. But the club maintained they had larger rights of ownership over him. He went to law, no matter that in the meantime Newcastle sold him to Arsenal (for £47,500). His Q.C. was Gerald Gardiner – the man who also defended the publishers of *Lady Chatterley's Lover* in 1960. Eastham won. Thereafter, a player could leave a club when his contract was over. That was proper. That it led to a situation where players demanded to leave if they felt irritated about their parking place was only the definition of another kind of tyranny. The £20 wage limit was shot to pieces. Johnny Haynes of Fulham was given £100 a week then and there. The players did not own the game, but they had come closer to power. The best of them, overnight, could feel rich, and might eventually be so. They were, therefore, that much harder to teach, discipline and manage.

There were bitter ironies. Ramsey himself had never earned more than the standard wage, or developed his lifestyle beyond lower middle-class aspirations. He was soon earning much less than his stars. He had players – outcasts of the British education system very often – who had money to burn. The new liberty of football players was only a means to the kind of lavish burn-out that ruined George Best (but which does not stop him from being the first hero of sports). Ramsey would be distressed by players who took big sums of cash to wear new boots in important games.

He was himself indifferent to money, as only lifetimes of strict economy can ensure. And in his age, football players became not just heroes, but television personalities, fashion plates, fringe figures in the entertainment world, sportscar owners, and louts who lived in stockbroker Surrey.

There were tensions between Ramsey and his players. He was far from a hedonist; he rebuked their urges to go off to pubs and clubs. He scolded their neglect of their bodies. He told them to train harder in drab privacy. He had been formed by the game when poor kids saw it as their best chance, short of boxing or crime, to make some kind of living. Alf Ramsey was a teenager in the 1930s; and his players were handsome young devils let loose on the England of the 1960s.

He was a revolutionary at the Football Association. He turned their house upside down. But he was also the end of an old order. He never could get on with a Jimmy Greaves, who talked back. He never could fathom a player like Denis Law, who was brilliant and only wanted to be more brilliant. Alf Ramsey had that wary and disappointed look of a haunted father. But his sons owed him so much.

HALF-TIME

At half-time, we gaze out on what is called the pitch – there is not much else to do. But 'pitch' is so remarkable and extensive a word, we might spend our lives watching and wondering. 'Pitch' means to put down a tent; it refers to the key in which music works, and allows that some people can have 'perfect pitch'; it is the crucial act of throwing the ball at home plate in baseball, and the skill that famously determines such contests – 'good pitching beats good hitting.' 'The pitch' is also the way in which in Hollywood or Hollywood-like situations, that idiot, the writer, tells his story to the faces who are money and go-ahead if they smile. 'To pitch' may also mean to fall forward, or to join the group effort as in, 'let's all pitch in'. It is a shot in golf; it can describe the angle of an aircraft in flight; it may be the known or claimed area that a beggar or busker has on a particular street. It is also, to quote Webster, 'any of various dark, tenacious, and viscous substances for caulking and paving, consisting of the residue of the distillation of coal tar or wood tar'. Pitch-black is the deepest dark; fever pitch is the height of excitement; and pitch-blende is the ultimate ore in which uranium and radium may be found. A pitcher is not just Bob Gibson or Dizzy Dean (a St Louis Cardinals hero, whose active career overlapped with that of Dixie Dean, the Everton and England centre-forward). A pitcher is also a jug, and something a South London kid sees at the movies.

Wembley, this day in July 1966, is already scarred and pitted: there are wounds of chocolate earth showing in the shiny green. These little flaws are like scratches in a movie screen that has served valiantly, from Buster Keaton's *Sherlock Jr* to Antonioni's *Blow-Up* (an important event in 1966). This is the Wembley where the Hungarians began re-education in 1953; it's also the arena for show-jumping finales and Billy Graham campaigns. This is the ground, the pitch where, in 1948, Barney Ewell ran second in the 100 metres, and yet today, as I write (December 12th 1995), the same Ewell, seventy-seven, has just had his second leg amputated. The first went two years ago.

If it is now close to 4 p.m. at Wembley on July 30th 1966, then it is 8 a.m. in San Francisco, where the day is dawning in the thought that Sandy Koufax may pitch for the Dodgers in a few hours at Candlestick. This is the Candlestick where, a month or so ahead, the Beatles will do their last live concert. And it is the place where more than twenty years later, after an operation for cancer in his arm, Dave Dravecky will come back to throw and win one more classic game before they have to take his arm off. And it is the place where, so many times, Joe Montana and Steve Young have led decisive, winning drives. The grass grows anew every year, but something essential of the pitch remains.

When my Dad came home it was on Friday evenings, and in the summer I would wait at the bus stop at the end of our road on the edge of the Common. I had a bat and a ball, and when he got off the bus (he was always on time after what must have been a two-hour journey, by coach, Tube and bus), we'd have a couple of overs each using two trees as wickets. For several years, there was no grass between those trees, just hard ground worn bare by cricket. That was in the 1950s. In the decades since, when I've returned, I find a lush grass grown back. Then one of the trees was gone, taken in some calamitous elm disease. No-one plays cricket there now. But in the 1950s, we worked that 16-yard pitch, with a hard ball and no pads, bowling fast, and sometimes driving the ball through the covers, across the cinder horse-riding track, so that it banged against the red steel sides of passing buses. And the conductor would yell out, 'Oy, watch it!'

It must have been testing for my father, close to fifty, because in those years I was growing and bowling faster all the time. Once or twice I hit him in the leg, and he'd hop and turn away for a while and tell me, over his shoulder, 'No, no, I'm fine.' And I recall a day when he drove the ball straight back at me – just 16 yards. I had no time for my fear to work, so the thunderous catch just stuck in my hands. The fire went up my arms. And he was walking towards me, aghast, afraid of what he might have done.

'I caught it!' I yelled.

'Good catch, lad,' he said. And he surely knew he might have killed me. We played with a hard ball, because that was cricket. Tennis-ball cricket was for sissies. The real ball had that glowing, deep red I've never seen anywhere else. Except in blood. I used to handle the ball for hours, polishing it, drawing my fingers across the varnished seams. Spinning it in the air so it hissed.

That Common where we played was Tooting Bec Common, which seemed an infinitely large place of play then. And it was all the larger for holding sway in dense suburbia. It had the horse-ride, boating ponds, a 100-yard-long open-air swimming pool, grass tennis courts, fields for grown-up cricket and soccer, and areas of thick wood. That was where, my Granny told me, Adolf Hitler was hiding out in 1945. You see, his body had not been discovered, or admitted to, then. So it was easy to believe the monster had escaped. This was probably not a sensible thing to tell a four-year-old, who sometimes drifted as much as ten yards away from his mother on the Common. But I believed her. I was in raptures as I searched. At four, I had so odd and innocent a view of the war, even if our house had been hit a couple of times by bombs – once with a fire in the roof, and once with such damage that several feet had to be lopped off the house.

The house we lived in was my Granny's – so my father had

left her, too, and I'm sure he gave her no more explanation than anyone else. He never made any pretence of liking her. The house had three floors, or flats, but it was open, with just one front door, and so the woman who lived alone on the top floor, a Miss Jane Davis (a member of the Dickens Society), had to come up through the two floors below. My mother and I lived on the middle floor, and my father when he came home. And my Granny had the ground floor, with the fine French windows that led out into the back garden. I have seen photographs of that garden before the war, one with my mother as a beautiful young woman, and it had been prettily cultivated then. But in the war, gardening stopped, because of bombs and damage, and the building site the war needed to repair the house. There was a shed at the end of the garden, overgrown, and supposedly the lair of rats. Rats then favoured the bombed-out houses. We had a black cat, Mackie, that killed a rat most nights.

It must have been more dangerous than I knew. The Common was split by the main railway line from London to the south coast; it was a target for German bombers. The streets I began to play in had many bomb sites, and there was one corner plot that had been obliterated. Pre-fabricated, temporary homes were put up there, and I believe they were still occupied in 1966. In many ways, the war ended very slowly.

Danger is a peculiar thing. I was devoutly looked after, an only child. But my first wife used to say that that had ruined me. Still, my mother raised me in a house that could have become rubble in an instant, in a country that might have been invaded. And she did that on very little money, while having to look after a mother-in-law she loathed, with a husband who had left her at the large moment of childbirth. She had secured orange juice for me, meat and eggs, at a time when those things were rationed. She also kept me safe in the thought that my father loved me. She did all she could to look after my body and my hopes. But maybe that was more dangerous than leaving my father and the house of his family. I still don't know, but I feel affected, and compromised, by that strange household. My Dad's weekends at home were fixed and splendid in routine. He never came back furtive or sheepish: he was my hero returned. In addition, he kept to a pattern that seemed to bespeak great confidence and reliability. Only gradually, I learned that the pattern came from his refusal, or inability, to listen to or heed anyone else. But I was its beneficiary.

He came home Friday nights for his supper. On the Saturday morning, he went grocery shopping with my mother, and when that was done, he went to the local stamp shop, for he was a collector, with many albums. The Saturday lunch was early enough to permit a sporting afternoon: that was either Chelsea at Stamford Bridge, or a local amateur team, Tooting & Mitcham United. But in the summer, the Saturday could be cleared away, with a picnic lunch assembled so that he and I could go to cricket, at Lord's or the Oval. In the 1950s, English county cricket was dominated by the Surrey team – essentially, it was Clark, Fletcher, Peter May, Constable, Barrington, Eric Bedser, McIntyre, Lock, Laker, Alec Bedser, and Stuart Surridge, the captain. They won the County Championship nearly every year, and they were my team. In the summer holidays, I would take the twenty-minute bus ride to the Oval on my own to see them. My father had elected to support Middlesex, and he especially believed in the excellence of Denis Compton (both Denis and his brother Leslie had played for Arsenal's Cup-winning side against Liverpool in 1950 – Leslie was also wicket-keeper for Middlesex).

We went to athletics and tennis, too, as special events. He took me to speedway, and then once, as a lark, we went to see an American Army game of baseball. We decided that it was ridiculous and impenetrable. Much later in his life, I told him we had been wrong. But he never yielded to that possibility. We went by bus to see Chelsea; we had no car. It was the 49 bus to Battersea Bridge and then a walk to Stamford Bridge. It was the 159 and an hour's ride to Lord's and any bus to the Oval. As for Tooting & Mitcham, we could walk there without any trouble. There came a time, when Tooting got to be a really good team, when we'd even follow them to away matches – to Sutton, Carshalton, Kingstonian, Woking, and even as I recall, north of the Thames, to see Hendon, Walthamstow Avenue and Wycombe Wanderers. I have half an idea that we even went to see them once at St Albans. Which leaves me wondering whether he had advised his woman there to be on such-and-such a corner at ten past two so she could catch a glimpse of us. No, it's more likely that he never told her.

On Sundays, we'd buy the papers: *The Dispatch*, *The Express*, *The Pictorial*, *News of the World*, *The Graphic*, and was there something called *Reynolds News*? (None of what you'd now call 'quality' Sunday papers.) But I perfected my reading on the sports reports, sometimes of games we'd seen. And he'd help me cut out pictures for a scrapbook.

Then we'd walk over to Mitcham, where my other grandmother, my mother's mother, lived. We'd take a ball, a tennis ball, and go the back way on side streets so that we could kick it along as we went. We practised moves and dribbling, and sometimes I'd be Laurie Reilly, the Hibernian centre-forward, whom I loved, and he'd be Frank Swift.

We'd have a cup of tea and a talk with Grandma and Bert, my grandfather. Then he and Dad would go to the pub for a beer, while I sat outside and had a lemon squash and a packet of crisps. We'd get the 115 bus home and be back for a big roast dinner just as 'Two-Way Family Favourites' was ending on the radio.

In the afternoon, Dad would read the papers, especially the *News of the World* – he was very serious about court reports. In the evening, he'd go to the pub and come back for a supper of sandwiches. My Granny would come up for that, and to avoid having to talk to her, he'd have the radio on with the current BBC serialisation of some classic novel.

The next morning he'd be gone before 7.00. You could set your watch by him. And it was years later before I saw how desperate the need for routine was. That was when my mother was dying from a brain tumour, and sighing all the time like breathing, and he still somehow expected a proper full roast lunch on the table at 1.00.

SECOND HALF

11

I dreamed last night of Denis Law. He wasn't doing anything much more than walk around the pitch, watching the comings and goings, with that twisted grin on his pale face, and his hair standing up like fire. He was amused to see the hash other players were making of things. He was tickled by the weird concert of mud, heavy boots and weary limbs. Denis Law used to laugh a lot on the pitch, and it was often evident that he was talking to other players, or talking to himself. And you could easily imagine that a foul, Scots mouth went with his wicked angel look. For if Denis Law was touched by genius, you knew that he responded to it like a wild horse feeling the first saddle on its bare back.

He was innately rebellious: he was James Dean cut with some mad, albino ballet dancer. He was as good as anyone I ever saw, and when it suited him very physical, very robust – all right, he could kick your lights out. He had violence in him, spite, a nastiness especially reserved for the English. And yet Denis Law, so slim of hip, so swift in the turn, could somehow look like a beautiful, dangerous girl. He was on fire with more than just football and his own instincts for it, he knew that soccer was also a war with the elements, with fate, in which the promise of a perfect round ball was offset by bumps in the ground, swirls in the wind and the occasional gracelessness of others. And he could look at a team-mate, as angry as the Queen of Hearts saying, 'Off with their heads!' But then he'd laugh, as if realising what a fatuous thing a game is. You could believe that Denis Law might have killed to win – or just walked off the pitch and gone away to Tahiti to watch the light.

Take the 1963 Cup Final, Manchester United versus Leicester City, a game in which Denis ran wild over the Wembley turf and seemed bent on humbling Gordon Banks, the Leicester goalkeeper. United were classes ahead. Denis had scored one goal. And then he made an extraordinary move, assassinating the defence, and rising to take the destined, headed goal from a Johnny Giles cross. He met it exactly. The ball sang through the air. Banks was a spectator. But the header hit the bar, and as the bemused Banks turned to watch, the ball landed neatly in his incredulous arms. Denis Law reeled, cried to the injured heavens, went down on the grass on his knees, and beat the ground with fury, and the sheer merriment of greatness being so thwarted. As Banks wrote about Law, in his own book, 'He could be arrogant, precocious, evil-tempered, hilariously funny and simply brilliant all in the space of a few minutes.'

And it was Law who dominated the England versus Scotland game at Wembley in April 1967, the first meeting of the old enemies since England had won the World Cup. England fielded their winning side but for one position (Greaves replaced Hunt). The Scots team was: Simpson, Gemmell, McCreadie, Bremner, McKinnon, Greig, McCalliog, Baxter, Wallace, Law, Lennox. Scotland won 3–2, and Law scored the first goal, with a killing second shot after Banks had only parried his first. It was a way of saying Scotland, in truth, were the world's best.

So I mention Denis Law just as a way of saying that in those early 1960s there were extraordinary characters on the football pitch, many of whom could not play for England. Law, famously, played golf that July 30th, refusing even to watch on television.

I must also mention Jimmy McIlroy, of Burnley and Northern Ireland, a masterly passer of the ball, a visionary ahead of his time, and the first player I ever saw who, with possession, turned his back on a defender and simply backed into him, the way basketball players will bring the ball up-court. Defenders were mystified. They could foul McIlroy, or try to come round the corner at him. When they did, he went the other way and laid the ball off to those Burnley greyhounds, Pointer, Connelly, Robson, Pilkington.

That great Spurs team of the early 1960s relied on at least four 'foreigners': the speed of Welshman Cliff Jones on the wing, along with his uncommon appetite for goals; the granitic severity of Scottish wing-half Dave Mackay; and his partner, Danny Blanchflower, of Northern Ireland. Blanchflower was a man who might have made a politician or a teacher. He could talk beautifully and sensibly, and he gave every indication of understanding a myriad things above and beyond soccer. But he was also a natural, easy leader of men on the field and a heartfelt maker of plays. Surely he talked to his players, too, and knew how to direct them. But they listened to him only because he could hold the ball when necessary, pass it exactly and play to his companions' skills. Then there was the Scottish inside forward, John White, who could find openings the way smart fish know that a net is just a collection of holes. Together, White and Blanchflower guided that Spurs team that won the Double in 1960–61:

Brown (Scottish)

Baker   Henry

Blanchflower   Norman   Mackay
(N. Irish)   (Scottish)

Medwin   White   Smith   Allen   Jones
(Welsh)   (Scottish)   (Welsh)

As if it needed improvement, that's the Spurs line-up which Jimmy Greaves joined next year. And Spurs might have lasted longer in glory, but Blanchflower hurt his knee, Mackay kept breaking a leg, and John White was killed by lightning on a golf course.

There are others I should mention: Ian St John, centre-forward for Liverpool and Scotland; Pat Jennings, the Northern Irish goalkeeper who came to Spurs and was, arguably, as good as Banks; Mike England, the Welsh centre-half. And then, in the 1964–65 season, there began to be word that Man United and that eternal Matt Busby had done it again, that they had found a kid from Northern Ireland as good-looking as the Beatles, who could take a game over. George Best could, when he wished or decided, take the ball past anyone. I remember the first time he came to the Bridge, and no-one could stop him or touch him. He ran with his head down, shoulders hunched, and his body seemed like the definition of balance. And he didn't cut his hair, so soon he looked like a real Beatle.

He was a star, like Law, like Greaves, like Bobby Moore, even. It may have been that these young men were now wealthy from television's increasing coverage of soccer. But they were also kids of the emerging 1960s: football gear became tight-fitting and shorts were cut high on the thigh. Denis Law may have looked fleetingly girlish, but girls and women were beginning to ask to go to football matches to get a look at the eyefuls, the little bits of terrific. Football began to be sexy – all of this was underway before the World Cup of 1966; and all of it was confirmed and accelerated by that victory. That's the real reason, I think, why Denis Law was worth watching, or dreaming about, just walking around doing that strut of his, being Denis. Letting anyone know that there was glory in just being out there, master of the pitch.

Something like this mood prevails at Wembley as the second half begins, and it is ushered in by a heavy rain that increases as play resumes. This rain is not just local, but English. A part of the old character of English soccer is that it endures and excels in heavy weather, in rain, ice and mud. Let Jerry try a taste of this! And as the rain comes down harder, there is a drum-beat chant of 'England! England! England!', more brutal and urgent than anything in the first half. The crowd smells blood in the rain, not just the dank stench of moisture or coats embedded with the old cigarette smells of seasons.

England's kick-off goes back to Stiles, and then to Moore. He passes out to Wilson, who slips the lunging challenge of Haller and moves downfield before crossing. That repartee, the small talk, of close passing is quickly re-established. Wilson's cross is low and awkward. Schnellinger bends to head it away. Ball snaps up the trifle, and slides Bobby Charlton free on the right of the penalty box. Charlton races on, with Schulz in attendance. Then he spills over as the ball goes out of play.

There is a great roar of outrage from the surly crowd: they 'saw' a penalty in Schulz's tackle. It is an understandable feeling, for Schulz may inadvertently have tripped Bobby. A Denis Law here would play to the crowd. He would be crucified in indignation. The crowd's noise would turn ugly. A referee might lose control, many might give a penalty. It is in the nature of Bobby Charlton that he allows no fuss. Instead, he calms the crowd with a quick shake of Schulz's hand as he races back into position. That Bobby, always reluctant to be a star or cause a scene.

Tilkowski's goal-kick is too weak to reach the half-way line – there is wind with the rain – and Ball heads it out of play. Schnellinger's throw goes to Emmerich, and then to Held, but Cohen takes it away. Another throw, by Stiles, goes to Bobby Charlton and back to Stiles. His high ball to Hunt is easily shepherded out of play by Weber.

There are a few more throws, as if play cannot escape the touchline, and then Ball, drawing back from the German defence, contrives to send a lovely short lock-breaking pass on to Cohen's forward run. It is a glimpse of Ball asserting himself, and of natural skill finding a way. Cohen is clear, so his feeble cross is worse than disappointing. But Germany cannot clear straight away. When they do, the aimless forward ball finds Jack Charlton alone in the centre circle. He breasts the ball down and is whistled for handling. Whereupon, Jack is as vehement as a Belfast Prot accused of Popishness.

The free kick goes to Beckenbauer, but Moore wins it easily – the Germans seem taken aback by the new English resolve. Moore gives it to Hurst, who passes to Peters, then, as Peters moves inside, Bobby Charlton crosses over behind him, going left. The German defence sways over to contain Bobby, and Peters passes sideways the other way to Stiles, clear on the right. Schulz makes the clearance, but only by putting the ball out of play. Stiles's throw-in goes to Hurst and then back to Stiles again, who is bundled out of play by Emmerich. Stiles gives the German a warning look, and there is again that edge in the air that suggests people must pay for their wrongs. Soccer crowds, let alone players, can become obsessed by injured innocence and injustice. This game has been clean so far, but both sides have the men who could put in the boot. The grass is wet and skiddy now, and no-one knows how to turn a wild skid into a hack better than Norbert Stiles.

England will not be shaken from the right flank. Yet again, Ball sends Stiles clear down the wing, compelling an emergency tackle from Schulz. Then Ball has the ball again, and he artfully draws away from the defence until he is fouled. Whereupon, he becomes pain's actor: the tension is building, and the crowd are being whipped up by these incidents. From Cohen's free kick, Moore heads down to Hurst. Jack Charlton is there on the eighteen-yard line, eager to push home the attack. But if he is there, who is guarding the heart of England's defence?

Quick as the thought, Germany clear. Held feeds Seeler, who edges it on inside to Haller, with Held racing forward. Haller passes as quickly as he can, but Held is judged to be half a step off-side. Maybe. It is a very close call and a warning blade at the heart of England's system.

'That was Jack going up!' moans my friend. 'What's he doing up there?'

'Getting excited,' I say.

'Give him a sedative, quick,' says my friend. But England are coming again. Moore is moving forward in space, inter-passing with Charlton. The ball goes to Wilson on the flank, who gives it inside again to Moore. His deep cross is out of Hurst's reach and bounds into Tilkowski's grasp.

'I should have taken a piss at half-time,' says my friend. The pressure is mounting.

12

One Saturday, my Dad and I had been to see Chelsea. It may have been in that far-fetched year, 1954–55, when they actually won the First Division. Chelsea in those days were something of a joke: they often played attractive football, but they never came close to winning anything. There was a very comfortable air at the Bridge about the losing. It was expected, and sardonically relished. Early leads in those days fooled no one. 'Hello,' people would say on the terraces, 'watch out!' And sure enough, Chelsea would squander that lead, contriving grisly and hilarious ways of giving up goals. 'That's Chelsea for you,' loyalists sighed on the way out of the ground.

But in '54–55, with a team no better than others, they took the championship itself:

Robertson

Harris   Willemse

Armstrong   Wicks   Greenwood

Parsons   McNichol   Bentley   Stubbs   Blunstone

We didn't really follow that side. By then, my school was Dulwich College, which had school on Saturday mornings and played rugby. For years, for me, that was the greatest failing in

94

the school. I played rugby, learned to like it, but I regarded it as a snob's game, the upper-class winter sport. My Dad had a joke, that rugby was the gentleman's game, and football the thinking man's sport. So I was often involved on Saturdays, and I sometimes played for the school, which meant coach trips to places like Mill Hill, Merchant Taylors' and Haileybury.

Anyway, we had been to this game – I have no other recollection of it – and we had walked all the way up the Fulham Road and the Old Brompton Road to catch the bus at South Kensington station. I don't remember anything about that walk, certainly nothing to prepare me for what happened.

We were waiting at the bus stop, and dusk was coming on. There were not many other people around; I believe there was no-one else at the bus stop. Now, I may have been doing something foolish, or chattering on about something that annoyed him – I don't know. I have no memory of it. But suddenly, he punched me very hard in the stomach.

"Ow 'ard?' asks my friend, all indignant.

'Very hard. I went down on my knees. I couldn't breathe. I thought I was going to be sick.'

'He hit you, just like that?'

'Just like that.'

'No-one came up and stopped him?'

'I'm not sure anyone saw.'

'South Ken, on a Saturday evening?'

'It does seem odd,' I admit. 'Maybe if anyone saw, they thought it was none of their business.'

'How old were you?'

'Thirteen?'

'And he was a grown man!'

'He wasn't tall.'

'Never mind, it's the principle.'

'He'd been a boxer,' I add.

'Bloody 'ell! He'd been a boxer and he's poking you one?'

'Just an amateur.'

'Still.'

'He worked for a time at Wimbledon Stadium – on the management side. And while he was there, there was a boxer, Tom Heeney, who was training to fight Max Baer – '

'Max Bloody Baer? Heavyweight champion?'

'Right. My father was only a lightweight, but Heeney liked him as a sparring partner because he was quick.'

'I hope Heeney unloaded on him.'

'Don't know. It was 1931 Heeney fought Baer – I've looked it up. Baer knocked him out in the third. My Dad would have been twenty-three.'

My friend is bemused. 'So what happened?'

'Well, the bus came along and we got on it. He helped me get on.'

'You ask him why?'

'He wouldn't say a word, the whole way home and ever afterwards. Never mentioned it.'

'He used to hit you a lot?'

'No, hardly ever. Never like this.'

You see, it was an unfair punch. I wasn't ready, wasn't even looking. And that was not like him. I wonder if some demon had sprung up in him that just thought to try it. Or had I said something that hurt him? Had he seen something or someone on the street that made him so sad he had to do something? Had he had some insight about his own failure, his trap, the horror of it?

'You're a sight too generous to him, mate, if you ask me.'

'Maybe.'

'And that was 1954 – nine years after your war is over – and he's still doing the weekend thing?'

'Right.'

'And you weren't mystified by that?'

'I was.'

'I bet you challenged him!'

'Perhaps, but I don't think so. I was scared to ask him.'

'You had every right!'

Of course, that's true. But I know now that I was afraid to disturb this absurd, ghastly situation. I think my mother was intimidated in the same way. I'd talked to her about it by then, and she'd said that it was just the way of things. That he preferred to live away, while coming home all the time to see us – because, she said, apart from anything else, he meant to keep the house we lived in, with his mother. Because she didn't die until 1959.

'And your mother didn't leave him?'

'No, she thought she wouldn't be able to manage.'

'She tell you about the other woman?'

'Not then.'

'So you thought he was living in St Albans on his own?'

'He always seemed very alone.'

As I said, he didn't hit me. Didn't really touch me: never hugged me or kissed me. Though I felt he loved me and knew I loved him. But there was violence in him, and it slipped out that twilight at the bus stop. I can only say that it had to do with a climate of fear, and the depression that came from that. Until I had to ask myself, why must one be depressed? Why not win?

'Win? How d'you mean?'

'I don't know how to put it – how to admit that I wanted glory and some feeling of joy and triumph.'

My friend looks at me. 'You should have hit him back.'

'Yeah,' I say. 'Killed him perhaps.'

He grins. 'Like you'd have polished off that Adolf Hitler, if you'd found him on the Common.'

'Right,' I say, cheering up.

Tilkowski throws the ball clear to Haller. He plays it inside to Overath, who gives it back to him. From inside his own half, Haller sends a long, probing ball down the centre where Held is off-side. This time beyond question. Jack Charlton and Moore exchange grins over the neatness of the trap.

The free kick goes to Stiles, by way of Hurst to Bobby Charlton, who slips it to Ball on the right. He, in turn, gives it outside to

Cohen, who is overlapping. The full-back is well covered. He doubles back and gives it to Stiles, whose deep cross is cleared away to the right by Schulz, to Overath in the corner. He then sends the ball across to Tilkowski.

The punt clearance is easily headed away by Jack Charlton. It goes to Stiles, and then Cohen, before the Germans take control in midfield. Schnellinger gives it to Haller, who passes it on to Held on the left. But Jack Charlton first tackles him, then guides him into the corner and ensures a goal-kick to England.

Banks's kick is strongly cleared by Weber. It goes to Emmerich, who has a minor tussle with Stiles in which the English player is called for a foul. Stiles is not of the same opinion: he bounces the ball high in dudgeon, but then acts contrition when the referee hurries to reproach him. The free kick goes to Haller, and again out to Held on the left. His cross is not very threatening, but Jack Charlton elects to take a gentle dive to head it away for a corner.

Haller's corner kick is well cleared by a Peters header, but the ball only goes to Schnellinger. He gives it to Overath, who finds Haller. He passes back to Schnellinger, who sends in a cross from the left, intended for Seeler. But Jack Charlton has him mastered in the air now. The German attacking energy seems reliant on Haller. Seeler has done very little this half. Emmerich is close to being a passenger. In short, Germany never seem to have enough attacking players forward. Overath and Beckenbauer are increasingly mindful of defensive duties.

From the English clearance, Haller fouls Ball. The free kick goes back to Banks, whose big punt is cleared by Schulz. But Peters picks up the ball and gives it to Bobby Charlton. He finds Moore, who sets Wilson free down the left. Wilson's cross is deceptive: at first, it seems headed for the goal, but it picks up a late outwards curl that forces Weber to head away. The ball goes to Overath, whose pass up the right wing to Seeler finds the German striker heavy-footed.

Wilson throws in to Hurst. The ball goes back to Wilson, who slips it across-field to Stiles. In turn, he gives a sweet pass from the outside of his right foot to Ball, who is increasingly busy and successful in finding space. Ball's cross reaches Peters a trifle late, so that the header goes high and wide. But Peters was clear, and greater accuracy – plus a similar authority in the air – could have made a goal like Hurst's.

Tilkowski kicks away very poorly, and is lucky to have Schnellinger gather the ball. He feeds Overath, who gives it to Beckenbauer, who is fouled. The free kick gets the ball to Haller, who sees the chance of a rapid forward pass to Seeler on the right. It is a smart idea, but the ball goes too quickly for Seeler, who seems increasingly disconsolate.

The rain has stopped now. But the softened surface is making for large divots, like commas in a text, and a few players are slipping. The weather makes a mistake all the more likely.

Moore takes the throw-in. It goes to Bobby Charlton, who gives it back to Moore. As he clears down the left, Moore slips, and the ball meant for Hurst goes out of play. Höttges throws it in, to Overath and so on to Beckenbauer. He passes to Schnellinger, who gives it to Held. But one more pass to Emmerich leads to an easy English tackle.

Ball takes the loose ball on. He passes to Bobby Charlton, who finds Peters midfield, about 25 yards out. Yet again, Peters tries a shot from there, and again it is harmless and wide. But England's dominance cannot be missed. They are playing like a side that feels the win is just a matter of time.

13

Then there was Tooting & Mitcham, who were not just the last bond I had with my father, but an unexpected glimpse of the paradise of winning. He was less interested in going to see Chelsea. I don't know why – perhaps, at his age, fifty by then, he began to be suspicious of the huge crowds. Not that there was as yet any hint of violence or, indeed, of anything less than a sweeping benevolence in those gatherings. In hindsight, I think that he may have been withdrawing in a larger way, making less effort, getting lazier or less impressed by things.

Or maybe it was just that Tooting hit a streak. They were then an amateur club. The theory was that the players were not paid, that they turned up every Saturday for the love of playing, with only their expenses covered. It likely wasn't so: there were cheerful jokes in the Tooting crowd about how the players came off the field and found a fiver in their street shoes. They deserved more.

For in the late 1950s, Tooting & Mitcham were putting together a very good team. They so dominated one league, the Athenian, that they were promoted to another, supposedly superior, the Isthmian – it befitted the code of amateurism to have these leagues known by ancient Greek names. Both leagues would have been better described as the London Suburban League. In the Isthmian League, for instance, Tooting & Mitcham competed with – forgive me, I still love these names – Wimbledon, Dulwich Hamlet, Wycombe Wanderers, Oxford City, Walthamstow Avenue, Barking, Woking, Bromley, Clapton, Ilford, Kingstonian, Romford, Leytonstone, St Albans City, and a club made mainly of ex-University players actually called the Corinthian Casuals. This was in the 1950s, not the 1750s.

As I said, Tooting had players: only a few years before, a very good but immensely conceited inside-forward, Dave Bumpstead, had been signed up by Millwall to play professional in the Fourth Division. By 1958, the club had a young goalkeeper in development, Alex Stepney, who would go on to play for Millwall, Chelsea, Manchester United and England.

But in the 1958–59 season, 'Toot' was special. They had mixed their own talent with some signings from other clubs:

Pearson

Harlow   Edwards

Holden   Bennett   Murphy

Grainger   Viney   Hasty   Slade   Flanagan

The star of that team was Paddy Hasty, from Northern Ireland, a small, rather slender-looking, ash-blond centre-forward who specialised in diving headers and scoring goals. But, at its own level of play, there wasn't a weak link in the team.

Then and now, the FA Cup was a competition that begins as the season begins, with the final, at Wembley, in May, ideally the last game played. The big teams of the First and Second Divisions only entered the draw after Christmas. The Third and Fourth Division teams came in in late November. Tooting were involved in September, when we beat Bromley 5–1 in a replay. We then beat Redhill 7–1, Sutton United 8–1, and Horsham 4–0. In the first round proper, on November 5th – with fireworks going off in the crowd – we played and walloped Bournemouth & Boscombe, of the Third Division, 3–1.

Every year, the Cup had a few giant-killing teams: amateur

sides that beat professional teams, even League sides. The gap in talent wasn't that great, and the smaller teams were always on fire with enthusiasm. And, if at home, they were probably favoured by an insane crowd and a bizarre pitch. Tooting's ground was fair enough, but there were amateur sides who had sloping pitches and infamous mud patches.

In the next round, we were drawn at home again, against Northampton Town of the Fourth Division. We beat them 2–1. In both these games, there had been no luck about it. Toot were the classier side. The reports in big papers made it clear that this was a side with a lot of talent, very well organised, and driven by a once-in-a-lifetime fervour in its crowd. Our ground held maybe 10,000 people – but if you were in the front row you could sometimes touch the players, or get a muddy kick in your face. Equally, walking to the ground, on Sandy Lane, off Mitcham Road, you might find yourself beside one of the players and able to have a chat. In other words, the support for the team was both epic and intimate – like the feeling in an American college or university when it has a great team.

The draw for round three, the first round with all the teams in the country, was made before Christmas. On January 10th, 1959, kick-off 2.15 p.m. – it had to be that early because there were no flood-lights at the ground, and you had to finish before dark – we would play Nottingham Forest, of the First Division. Forest then were not a famous or glamorous side, but they were authentic First Division.

There was a frenzy in that little bit of south London. Tickets were very hard to get. I went to the ground one evening in the middle of the week, queued for hours, and got two. No-one was allowed more than two. One for me, one for Dad. It then turned out that January 10th was not one of his weekends home. I shamed him with a withering glance. Well, all right, he'd see what he could do. And it turned out that, yes, he'd be home.

The build-up was frantic. On Boxing Day, playing Bromley, and suffering our first defeat in three months, we lost goalkeeper

Wally Pearson to a broken jaw. There were rumours locally that he could be wired up, that he might be able to play still. The local paper, *The Streatham News*, which appeared every Friday, covered the event as if it were the Olympics.

The day came. Pearson was unfit. Reserve Ray Secker would play in his place. There had been a lot of rain, then a freeze: the pitch would be, variously, icy, muddy, and dangerous. So much of English soccer is played in marginal and hostile conditions and maybe that's why force has always been valued more than ball control.

My Dad and I got there hours early to have a great spot on the terraces. By the time the teams came out, you couldn't move. There were over 14,000 there that day. The Forest players loomed so large – the half-back line of Whitefoot, McKinlay and Burkitt. The forward line: Dwight, Quigley, Wilson, Gray, Imlach. I felt absolutely sick to the point of throwing up with the nerve of thinking we could play them. Yet the Forest players looked tense.

The next forty-five minutes were the greatest in my life to that point – I was close to eighteen – and I'm not sure they've been beaten. We handled them. We could do it. We had the skills, the touch, the blunt force when needed. They were a very nice side, no question, and they knew more than we did. But we weren't giving them time to remember it, and we were out there playing football. Paddy Hasty hit the bar, and Denzil Flanagan was about to put the rebound away when he slipped.

After twenty minutes, with the Forest defence in tatters, Albert Grainger strode through would-be tackles and drove the ball into the net. Twenty minutes later, Ted Murphy volleyed in a shot from 40 yards and there was the net in the Forest goal bulging to keep it in. I can remember the serge texture of my Dad's black coat as I beat my hands on his back with exultation, and his delighted face – I never saw him wilder or happier – turned to look at mine. It must be great to be a player, but to be a fan at such a moment shapes life. Half-time and we led 2–0.

Of course, they play two halves. Forest came out after half-time more settled and determined. And maybe Tooting had gone mad with the joy. After twelve minutes, Ted Murphy misplayed a back pass to the keeper, and the ball went in. He had scored for both sides.

2–1, with thirty or so minutes to play. We were tiring, they were gaining confidence. So we tried to hold out. About ten minutes from full time, referee Warnke gave a penalty against us when the ball hit Murphy – he was doomed! – in the chest, in the hand, in the life force. Who knows? The award was disputed. Later, some Forest players said they thought the penalty was undeserved. Murphy said the ball hit him in the chest. He was weeping. 'I don't tell lies,' he said – something no-one would have thought to say ten years later. Billy Gray scored from the penalty. 2–2. And so it remained at full time. Forest had survived. They clutched at our players to congratulate them, but you could feel the relief.

There would be a replay, at Nottingham, during the next week. But then winter descended. The Forest pitch was unplayable. The match had to be postponed twice – until January 24th. No-one really thought Tooting could win away, yet 2,000 of our fans made the journey. My Dad and I did not go. I had school. The day before that replay, the flamboyant motor-racing driver Mike Hawthorn was killed in a road accident on the Guildford by-pass. He lost control on a curve, going too fast, hit a lorry and struck a tree. He was dead when they took him out of his 3.4 Jaguar. It was a bad omen. At Forest, with Wally Pearson back in goal, we lost 3–0, in front of 42,000, an honourable defeat and a fair result.

And Nottingham Forest went on all the way to Wembley and won the Cup Final, 2–1, against Luton Town.

I had never known the jubilation of that first half, never been so close to so extraordinary a victory. In the local papers, the sports writer said it was a good thing it was all over. The glorious Cup run had been too much for a small side with a modest organisation. And it's true, you have to learn how to win at the big time. The strain told on Tooting: their season floundered. I loved them, and love them still in their black shorts and black-and-white-striped shirts, like Newcastle United, but I gradually gave them up after the run. I wanted that ecstasy, and I suppose I guessed that Tooting would never have it again. I wanted it at the top level. Chelsea for me.

But never forget that we had Forest – who never had a worse moment in the Cup that year – 0–2 down at half-time when they'd have sold their grannies for a guaranteed draw.

Tilkowski taps the goal-kick to Weber, takes the touch return and throws out to Overath. He then carries the ball forward, slowly, on a diagonal, before giving it to Schnellinger. His pass forward is beaten away by Cohen. Schnellinger recovers, and passes to Overath, who gives it to Beckenbauer. He passes to Seeler, who holds off a challenge from Hunt, and slides the ball away down the left to Held. Jack Charlton covers his thrust, and concedes a corner, with Stiles waiting as a back-up.

Held takes the corner, with Ball as close as he can get. The kick curls away from the goal and then, for once, Beckenbauer beats Bobby Charlton for it and moves in on goal. He is on the arc, his left foot poised – more dangerous than he has seemed all match – but then the shot trails away harmlessly.

Banks's punt bounces all the way to Schulz on the edge of his penalty area. His clearance is not well-timed and the ball goes out of play to his left. Cohen's throw-in goes to Jack Charlton, and then to Moore, who plays it on by way of Peters to Hurst. But Schulz clears it up again. He sends it upfield to Höttges, who seems to subdue the ball with his hand. The referee, very close, sees no offence and the crowd is soon singing 'What a Referee!' Haller begins another attack, and finds Emmerich in a promising position, but he then fires away a 'pass' to an empty corner of the field. Wilson retrieves it and gives to Moore, whose deep ball is flicked on. But Schulz is not to be beaten that way today. He passes to Overath, who swaps the ball back and forth with Schnellinger, before giving it to Held. Beckenbauer takes over and gives a neat pass to Seeler, who is unceremoniously dumped by Moore – not to be slipped twice. Moore's courtly hand to Seeler afterwards suggests the professionalism of that foul.

Beckenbauer tries to blast the free kick. But it bounces back off an English player to Overath. He puts in a lovely, drifting cross to Seeler, far on the right, whom England are trying to play off-side. Seeler is clear, but Banks easily takes his cross.

The keeper throws out to Bobby Charlton on the right, who gives it to Cohen coming up fast outside him. Cohen makes like a winger, but Beckenbauer tackles him tidily and puts the ball out of play. The throw-in sets up Cohen with a cross that the Germans fend away to their right, where the ball goes out of play. Wilson throws in to Moore, whose deep ball is headed down by Hurst, so that Peters can take a first-time shot – way over the bar.

14

When someone on the verge of eighteen is shouting himself hoarse and day-dreaming to the point of jay-walking over the story-book raptures of Tooting & Mitcham United football club, there might be a case for saying he needed broader horizons. But I had them; I was being very well educated at Dulwich College where I was doing History, English Literature and Latin for A-Level, aiming at Oxford. I was deep in Namier's eighteenth century; I was learning rolls of Milton, Wordsworth and Gerard Manley Hopkins by heart; I was directing a one-act version of Shaw's *St Joan*; I was discovering the National Film Theatre through its first Ingmar Bergman retrospective; I was seeing every movie I could as well as every football and cricket match. And I was having an affair, a love affair, my first, with a quite remarkable, brave, funny, smart and romantic girl from James Allen's Girls School, the 'sister school' to Dulwich College. I always wondered what the governors of both schools supposed was going to happen if eighteen-year-olds were raised on poetry, drama and the sporting life in two fixedly single-sex establishments side by side. And I suppose their answers would have been along the lines of, 'In Dagenham, I presume.' Or, as the Dulwich school motto put it, translated from the Latin, 'Let the glory be given to God alone.'

Before prudes and purists let out the moan, 'What has this got to do with 4–2 and *one* soccer match?' let me just remind you –

'Glory' – our secret subject, the passion. You see, July 30th 1966 is one climax among many, but a very appealing one, because it comes before most of the damage and the dark consequences to an English revolution that, luckily for me, or unluckily, coincided with my coming-of-age. It was the one moment in my life when I felt – without shame or irony – the code that had been drummed into me, all my life, that it was indeed terrific and special to be English. As opposed to a handicap.

Philip Larkin (a man not without Ramsey-ite traits) published 'Annus Mirabilis' in 1967, but it speaks to the undeniable sexual charge in the years I am talking about,

> Sexual intercourse began
> in nineteen sixty-three
> (Which was rather late for me) –
> Between the end of the *Chatterley* ban
> And the Beatles' first LP.

'Sexual intercourse' is rather the librarian's term, I think, the necessary way of looking up 'gold' in the index to the treasure house. And Larkin's parenthetical is a tender, self-mocking admission of how he may have been somewhere between a wistful scholar and a morose dirty old man (to have been late for that wonder must have been as galling as being a great player compelled to retire just as the maximum wage agreement was abandoned), but Larkin is right about the timing and the influences: the Beatles' first LP *was* called 'Please Please Me', and girls in the audience knew just what those clamant Mersey voices meant – one soft, one abrasive – as if to say, you might satisfy Paul, but John would be hard for ever. The Beatles' music was soundtrack to a sexual revolution, enabled by birth control – and it was the accompanying music to the great surge in British soccer. Often played in the hour before kick-off.

But 1963 still had problems with what to call *it*. It wasn't until November 13th 1965, on a late-night television show, that

Kenneth Tynan said, live, in front of Robert Robinson and Mary McCarthy, 'I doubt if there are very many rational people in this world to whom the word "fuck" is particularly diabolical or revolting or totally forbidden.' Of course, there was a frenzy of diabolised indignation, led by that most stubborn stopper of all time, Mary Whitehouse. (By the way, just as I see Ms Whitehouse as for ever stuck in the Craven Cottage mud of late January, I always want to make Tynan an honorary left-winger, for the Corinthian Casuals, no doubt, in a garish purple silk shirt, coughing as he runs, doodling the ball round censorious tackles. What a team Monty Clift and Ken Tynan might have made, rich in droll, not to say lewd, excursions.)

The exact place then to say 'fuck' officially in Britain was on the late-night BBC programme. Of course, late-night meant going on broadcasting after 11 p.m., a manoeuvre already tinged with wickedness. But the BBC in those days was a sublime, insouciant instrument of education and change, and part of the variegated team that was helping to make the country half-way grown up. I'm not sure how many episodes of *That Was The Week That Was* or *Z-Cars* I'd want to watch today (though the latter may hold up surprisingly well), but I know that in the early 1960s both were vital to the notion that there might be room to make fun, even malicious fun, of official hypocrisies, including God, patriotism, the Empire and the Royal Family, just as there was a way to use the work of modern policemen to show us the grim solitude and hardship of many lives, not to say the kind of banal horror that would be revealed in the Moors Murder Case. So long as we're not forgetting, and trying to remember, let's note that Myra Hindley and Ian Brady were sent to jail for the torture and murder of children only a couple of months before the big match at Wembley.

And at the same time, the young women of the country agreed to show off more of themselves. You can say that that 'fashion' was, as Mary Quant and her fellows argued, part of the glorification of the new woman, proud of her body, her beauty, determined to be free or unconstricted, defiant to stuffy conventions, ready for the new, and so on and so on. The new clothes were also a business that all the social reformers in rags wanted to sell. And in that first ecstasy of swinging London, I fear, the new styles were also a way in which young women – and sometimes not so young – were conned into putting themselves on display and making their availability evident. Almost like an advertisement. The styles were far from feminist. They were a blatant playing to male fantasies in which women became 'birds' or potential trophies.

So you saw those clothes everywhere, on the street and the Tube, but they were the costume of the wives, girlfriends and mistresses, the patient, largely silent, eternally pliant beauties in the ongoing news coverage of the Beatles and the Rolling Stones. They were the look of Jane Asher and Marianne Faithfull, who were then like chic, cool concubines, waiting to be discarded. The 'Satisfaction' the Stones howled for was very, very male.

And no-one, yet, complained.

It was also the way Christine Keeler looked – and it was on June 4th 1963 that John Profumo resigned from the Tory government because he had lied to the House of Commons about his relationship with her. That tiny, fatuous scandal brought down a government, and a self-consciously classical leader, Harold Macmillan, more or less because it exposed the way in which toffs, ministers and so on were having it off with dolly birds, and then acting as if they were still statues of probity. The Profumo case was a proof that satirical minds were on the right track. And Christine Keeler – with the flat, carnal, enigmatic look of Anna Karina in Jean-Luc Godard's films – was an ideal pin-up for the age: a wanton and a victim, horribly close to what the innocent Cliff Richard in 1959 had called a 'living doll'. Miss Keeler was hounded, but she was an icon and a fashion model. You can see her look all through the early 1960s: it's the stunned, lovely look that was expected of birds. Two decades later, Lady Di still had it.

You can see that look in the models whom the David Hemmings photographer character treats like shit in *Blow-Up*, which opened a few months after our great game and which was filmed in London in the summer of the World Cup. That very cool film is a heightened but unerring record of, and an austere commentary on, so many things about England at the time: the stress on style; the fascination with the arbitrary; a city of new music and clothes, and of glassy-eyed women who wait for a man's camera to shoot them; and those two groupies who gleefully let Hemmings strip them of their short dresses and their coloured tights until the audience gets little glimpses, snatched sights, of their pubic hair, and on a fade-out, they let themselves be fucked.

Blow-Up also has its game, of course, the game people play – tennis without the balls. That winked at the current notion that game-playing was *the* human sport (Eric Berne's *Games People Play* was a best-seller in 1966). But it also warms to such fancies as Ken Tynan and Monty Clift in left-wing partnership for some team, and the recurring, step-by-step, commentary I am making, or the dance I am memorialising, of a game that took place thirty years ago, a game set in time.

Tilkowski punts away on a ground that now looks puckered and torn as if shots had been fired at the soft surface. Seeler tries to flick the ball on, but it races towards the England goal-line where Wilson retrieves. He clears away to Moore, who carries the ball up the English left wing, looking more than ever commanding. He gives it to Hurst, who passes somewhat awkwardly across-field to Peters, who has to stretch, and beat Emmerich, to keep the ball. Bobby Charlton is moving outside him down the right, and Peters slips him the ball so that Bobby can cross it. Tilkowski jumps nervously and punches the ball away to his right.

He gives it to Schnellinger, who launches a very long cross-field ball, deep to the German left, to Held, who is diligently tackled by Cohen. But his clearance bounces on to Overath, who gives it back to Held. Then his cross is guided away by Moore, who passes to Ball moving up on the left. He slips it to Bobby Charlton, who is nicely robbed by a Beckenbauer moving back swiftly. Beckenbauer then sends it to Held, who passes to Overath out on the left. He returns it to Beckenbauer, who is generally holding to the middle of the field. He sends it farther right to Schnellinger, who puts in a long, booming shot over the bar.

England move out again – whenever possible (here is the old Ramsey) their goal-kicks work by short throws, so that possession is maintained. Moore carries the ball and gives to Stiles, who feeds Wilson coming up fast and strong on the left wing. His cross draws Tilkowski far from goal. Hurst is there, leaping and aloft, and again the German keeper pats the ball away – to Peters, who tries another first-time shot. It is wide, but Tilkowski seems incapable of dominating the air.

The goal-kick, to the right, is touched out of play by Stiles. Seeler takes the throw-in and the ball reaches Overath. He gives it laterally left to Weber. His pass to Schnellinger goes, by way of Held, back to Weber, moving up the left. But his cross is no great test for Moore.

The ball is loose in midfield for a while, but then England take control again. Bobby Charlton sets Ball free up the left. He sends a short, sideways pass to Peters, who immediately and with great vision sends the ball back to Hunt at the corner of the six-yard box. Hunt turns on it, and for an instant has Weber beaten, but then that excellent German defender recovers and knocks the ball out of play.

The throw-in gives Ball the chance of putting in a centre, but the ball goes over the German goal-line before he can hit it. Yet again, Tilkowski gives the goal-kick to a defender, Schulz, then picks up the return and punts away. As it lands, on the right, Wilson is whistled for pushing Seeler. Beckenbauer strokes the free kick quickly to an advancing Haller. But his cross is easily headed away by Jack Charlton. Moore then passes to Bobby Charlton, who is again beaten by Beckenbauer, who sends it up the right to Haller. He crosses into the oncoming rush of

Seeler, but Banks is entirely confident in being there first and punching the ball away. That clearance goes out to Emmerich, whose fumbling effort leads to a struggle for control between Beckenbauer and Peters from which Beckenbauer emerges in charge. He is looking better all the time, yet somehow he is guarded, as if under the burden of essentially defensive duties. In addition, the Germans seem weary of actually penetrating the English defensive alignment.

So Beckenbauer passes across-field – not into the English ranks – to Haller. He gives back to Beckenbauer, who now tries Schnellinger. He moves it upfield to Held, who puts in a shot – blocked by Cohen. Then Held takes the rebound towards the goal-line where Moore and Cohen guide the ball away for a corner.

Held's corner comes deep to Beckenbauer, who tries a shot. But Wilson knocks it clear, and Bobby Charlton moves on it, quickly enough to fool a covering Beckenbauer. He slips the ball on to Hunt, out on the left, and his persistence draws a foul from Overath. The free kick is taken with alacrity by Moore, for he has seen English players hurrying up on the right. This is very like the situation of the English goal, and the well-placed kick is headed downwards and only just wide by Jack Charlton, who feels no anxiety about joining the attack. We are twenty minutes and more into the second half. There is another quarter of regular time left, and no-one can have doubts about England's dominance.

15

In just that window of opportunity, or insinuation, that Philip Larkin spied for sexual intercourse, Chelsea went through their own dramatic spasm – a fall and a rising – that changed their sense of themselves as a football organisation. So, for me, it wasn't just that romance was in the air – along with the discovery of Godard, Nabokov, and American cinema – Chelsea had suddenly become something they had never been before, not even in their championship year, urgent, sexy, ambitious and modern. In the late 1950s, they had been an entertaining but ineffectual team, amiably led by Ted Drake, the old Arsenal centre-forward. They had relegation scares, but they had Jimmy Greaves as a salvation and a crowd attraction. To see that crew-cut kid from 1957 onwards was worth the price of admission. He played inside-forward, yet he scored more goals than centre-forwards: hat-tricks, or even fours and fives a few times, knifing through battleship defences, roaming the field, and showing an extraordinary, innate ability for seeing goal chances, that was both cruel and yet very practical. He dribbled the ball, beating men – just like the great Matthews and Finney – yet he was most himself when darting into a small space and striking in one short blow, hardly needing to control the ball, hammering it in. He finished things, when there had been no thought of a goal before he noticed it, and seized it. As a Chelsea Junior – and Drake's highest achievement was in building boy teams that would flower after he had gone – Jimmy once scored 114 goals in a season. Boys have to have goals and Greaves began to change the Chelsea crowd so that it shifted from being romantic and stoic to sensationalists expecting their fix.

In the spring of 1961, the rumour spread that Greaves was going to leave Chelsea – this was one result of the players' new contractual liberty. He was going to Italy, to A.C. Milan. He played his last game at the end of April, and scored all 4 goals in a 4–3 win. The fans had begged him to stay, but he was getting £15,000 in the Milan transfer, and he was a finisher. Except that he hated Italy. For Milan, he was double-marked by defences that also had a zone coverage with sweepers. He grew frustrated and homesick. He scored 9 goals in 14 matches, and then Milan agreed to return the wayward and immature kid to England. Spurs and Chelsea wanted him, and Jimmy chose Spurs.

'It was the making of him,' says my friend at Wembley.

'Maybe not in Ramsey's eyes,' I answer, unwilling to give up the argument.

'How d'you mean?'

'Alf likes loyalty.'

He nods, and says, 'And Alf never got none of that Eyetie money.'

Greaves may have guessed that Chelsea was going in the wrong direction – certainly not the same direction as Spurs. For in the next season, despite continued success for the youth team, and the arrival of a very different kind of manager, Chelsea were relegated. The full horror was made clear in a game, late in the season, when Chelsea still had an outside chance, and goalkeeper Peter Bonetti, his elbow injured, lay stretched out and writhing in his own goal area.

I doubt the new manager was anything but secretly elated. Teach them a lesson. Tommy Docherty had been a tough Glaswegian wing-half with Preston and Arsenal, and when he came to Chelsea first he was a player-coach under Ted Drake. He was always a hard, funny, caustic talker, someone who could inspire and get the loyalty of kids, and someone who had a vision of cohesive, close-passing, fast-running play that actually exceeded Docherty's own nature as a player. But he was also abrasive, volatile, quick-tempered, and insecure enough so that he might slap down the very kids he had made a gang out of. In his way Docherty acted like a bit of a gangster, one of the lads, then suddenly wary that the gang might betray him. To say the least, he was the most important character on the Chelsea side – he was the manager as star, headline-maker and self-destructive tyrant. He did a wonderful job with the team, and he raised everyone's temperature.

So, for 1962–63, we were in the Second Division with the clear purpose of making an immediate escape. It was a season of unbearable melodrama in which Chelsea took a big early lead, ran into a terrible despair, and then scrambled at the end to get second-place promotion. Of course, the autumn had other melodramas: it was the time of Russian missiles in Cuba, of Kennedy's ultimatum, and the fortnight in which it seemed the ball might burst, taking out the pitch, the crowd and everything else. You wondered if you were seeing your last match, or whether you'd see the whole match. Not that there was anything to be done. London mocked the televised reports of American civil defence preparedness. If we were scared, and we were, there was some comfort and encouragement to drink up in the thought, the promise even, that if 'it' happened, it would be all over in four minutes, or was it nine? Anyway, as quick as sex. And Chelsea kept banging the ball in the net of lesser teams like Grimsby, Rotherham, and Huddersfield.

Docherty had the best of a new generation of Chelsea kids, with a few seasoned players signed up from elsewhere. It was a team that captured the Bridge fans, and made them fiercer against all enemies. I'd never known a Chelsea crowd as determined or as ready for anger as the one that watched:

1–1

Bonetti

Shellito   McCreadie

Venables   Mortimore   Upton

Murray   Tambling   Bridges   Moore   Blunstone

Bonetti was fit again, and so agile and daring. Shellito then, before recurring knee injuries, was ahead of George Cohen. McCreadie, from Scotland, was languid yet hard. Venables – 'Tel' already – was a favourite, and sometimes a head so full of ideas it only showed up his physical limits. Upton was a blunt instrument. Mortimore was an ex-amateur. Murray and Blunstone were pure wingers. Graham Moore was a lovely, slow, constructive player (if a touch timid). Tambling was the new Greaves, or our best shot at it. And Bridges was a glorious sprinter, whose abandoned running forgave many lapses when he actually caught up with the ball. But not all.

There was also the winter that season which began – as I recollect – in a snowstorm on Boxing Day and meant that Chelsea hardly played for six weeks because of frozen pitches and the cast-iron snow. Then, as they came back, they faltered. The chief rivals for promotion were Stoke City and Sunderland, and there were two key matches towards the end of the season. Stoke came to the Bridge on May 11th – with a crowd of 66,000. The Stoke team was the opposite of Chelsea, they were veterans united: it included Eddie Clamp, once of Wolves; Jimmy McIlroy; the old Blackpool player, Jackie Mudie; Dennis Viollet; and, fory-eight-year-old, frail and silver-haired, Stanley Matthews. And they beat us, 1-0.

Never should have happened. Chelsea should have found a way to run the old legs ragged. But Tel on that day couldn't outwit McIlroy. It seemed a lost cause. The following Saturday we had to go up to Sunderland – nothing but a win there would do, but Roker Park was a tough place to play. Docherty gambled. He put Upton at centre-forward and slotted Derek Kevan in beside him. And he told them to put it about a bit – as Roker fans saw it, Chelsea played filthy. Upton's place at left-half was filled by another new kid, Ron Harris, not yet qualified as 'Chopper'. It was an ugly game, and we won 1–0 from a goal scored by another piece of Docherty inspiration. The old Spurs schemer, Tommy Harmer, had been on the books most of the season, but his style didn't work with Bridges and the gang. Harmer was a tiny craftsman, so slight that when he did tricks you couldn't help but feel how heavy the ball was. Anyway, little Tommy scored that one goal – and he never scored goals. It was in a goalmouth mix-up, and reports said it went in off his thigh or his stomach. Chelsea's story was that he scored with his jock-strap, having just seen a nice Sunderland girl on the terraces. Poke it in, Tom! You couldn't help it somehow, there was a crude mix of sex and violence getting into the game. A few days later came the Portsmouth match – 7–0 – and we went up, with Stoke.

A month later, no more, I was at Lord's for one day of one of the great Test matches: England versus the West Indies of Hall and Griffith, a day on which Ted Dexter made 70 in the middle session of the day, putting the terrifying fast bowlers to the sword. One of the most spectacular innings I have ever seen. Then I went to Barcelona for much of the summer, and when I came back I fell in love. Never a dull moment.

Not for the first time, description resumes with Tilkowski facing a goal kick: there is a pattern of English attacks that is making a rhythm to the game. He side-foots out to Schulz, who taps it back so that the keeper can throw it to Haller, who has fallen back into what is really a right-back position. He gives it to Overath, who lays the ball back to Weber so that he can pass back to Haller. Inching forward, the build-up goes to Overath again and so to Beckenbauer who, for once, prettily side-steps Bobby Charlton. He is in a promising position, but as if tired mentally he merely passes the ball directly to Cohen.

Cohen's clearance is mis-timed: it reaches Schnellinger and bounces back. But Cohen recovers and gives it to Ball, who lays on a nice crossfield pass to Peters. No-one now is running as eagerly as Ball, who seems to feel his strength is outlasting the Germans'.

Peters' shot is blocked, and bounces out to Haller, who passes to Held. But the attack is thwarted when Cohen knocks the ball back to Banks not much less sharply than a shot. Banks throws it out to Stiles, who pulls the ball over to Wilson on the left. His cross passes over a group of players where Schulz seems to nudge Hunt off-balance, just as the English player is about to jump. In response, Hunt gives a look of mortification worthy of comedian Eric Morecambe.

The ball goes over to the German left, where Held gathers it and launches himself forward, only to be stopped by Jack Charlton, who responds with a similar lone forward foray, passing English players standing nearly still but ready to let a reckless runner pass by. In turn, Jack's drive – surprisingly fast – ends in Haller's tackle. Then Haller leaves the ball to Schnellinger and himself runs forward to take Schnellinger's pass. But as it arrives, so Haller is . . . clipped, brushed, shaken, or knocked in the thigh by the obdurate Stiles? It is not quite clear. Haller rolls over in a tumble and gets up to show – lifting the hem of his shorts – his ravaged thigh. Stiles is incredulous, aghast, stupefied. The referee decides a foul has been committed, and Alan Ball comes in to make sure that Stiles and Haller shake hands. It wasn't that much, yet one feels a readiness for violence, as if – had he been less tired – Stiles might have really crocked Haller.

The German free kick goes by way of Schulz and Schnellinger out to Höttges on the right. He tries to release Seeler down the wing, but Seeler can only return the ball for Höttges to cross it. Cohen clears it comfortably towards Bobby Charlton, but Haller harries him and puts the ball out of play.

Cohen throws in to Bobby Charlton, who tries to set Cohen up in a position to cross the ball. But Schnellinger and Schulz engineer it back to Tilkowski. Stiles takes this deep ball, but can only kick it out of play. He seems very weary.

Höttges throws it to Schulz, whose forward pass to Seeler is beautifully beaten out by Moore who then moves forward. He gives it to Bobby Charlton and keeps coming forward. Bobby gives it to Ball, who feels Moore moving up outside him to his left. Ball makes to cut in, but then passes back across his body to Moore, who first times it back in a threatening cross. Hurst nods this on for Bobby Charlton, who is blocked only by a violent collision between Beckenbauer and Tilkowski that leaves both Germans on the ground, with the keeper clutching the ball.

The trainer comes on for a significant stoppage. Beckenbauer gets to his feet, holding his head, while Tilkowski stays in a heap.

'That goalie of theirs,' says my friend, 'he's ready to get hurt.'

It's true. Tilkowski seems caught in self-pity. But he gets up, cradling his jaw, and the game goes on. Yet again, England mount an attack. Stiles gives it to Moore, who passes to Wilson out on the left. Weber heads away the cross to Overath, who can only put the ball out of play.

Wilson throws to Moore, who feeds it back to Wilson. He gives it to Peters, who crosses – time and again, now, England are able to finish their attacks. The ball passes over Hurst and falls to Bobby Charlton, racing in on the right. His first-time, right-foot shot goes across the face of the goal and just beats the far post.

'These Jerry are getting bloody lucky!' says my friend – his face hungry for vengeance.

Tilkowski has another goal-kick to take.

16

I have three children who were all born in the 1960s – between the end of the *Chatterley* case and the 1966 World Cup – and I argue with them over just how real and exciting the thing called the 'Sixties' in London was. I tell them about how much was going on in, say, 1963, with Francis Bacon and Lucian Freud working at a peak, and with David Hockney a year out of the Royal College of Art and off on his first trip to Los Angeles. Think of that as a half-back line – Hockney, Bacon, Freud! And the children tell me I'm just a victim of the big myth, so calm down.

Parents and children have a hard time discussing history. The talk so easily slips into battle. And these kids have their grievance: they are the children of divorced parents, so maybe the much-vaunted Sixties in London – that foolish 'swinging' thing – was just an excuse for reckless irresponsibility. And, of course, it was: the freedoms worked and were meaningful to the extent that they were revenge on food rationing, austerity, guilt, silence, discretion, hypocrisy, denial, and the way of life in which your father also lived in St Albans, but it was never mentioned, let alone visited.

My son, Mathew – the one who saw his play ball rattle the fire irons when Haller scored – is now a university professor in history, and he likes to pour learned, cool water on my nostalgia, to the effect that it is all taken out of proportion, inflated by self-serving myth-makers, and flat-out exaggerated.

'The statistics don't support it, Dad,' he tells me sadly – he is sad to have so wayward a father. But then a week or so later, I meet an American friend, Greil Marcus, and it turns out that he and his wife, Jenny, honeymooned in London in June 1966, and he says, you'd better believe it, London then was amazing. They'd buy something on Carnaby Street one day – and next day the style had changed! They'd go to a pub in Brixton and there were the Yardbirds playing live!

And I can hear my son sighing at these middle-aged men and their exclamation marks.

So I breathe deeply and try to make the honour list calmly – movies like *The Servant, Lawrence of Arabia, Tom Jones, Darling, Billy Liar, The Pumpkin Eater, Repulsion, Morgan: A Suitable Case for Treatment, Blow-Up*; the mounting success of British soccer in European competitions; Spurs smashing Atletico Madrid to win the European Cup-Winners' Cup in 1963; West Ham beating Munich 1860 in the same competition two years later – and the feeling that the best of British soccer was getting back to a world level; the television!; the clothes!; the new music!; the theatre!; the – '

'Don't go on so,' says my younger daughter Rachel, 'it just makes us feel bad that we missed it.'

But, of course, they didn't miss it; 'it' made them, and surely helped give birth to them.

I came back from Barcelona that summer of 1963 in time for the fifth Test, at the Oval, between England and the West Indies. But I saw none of the play there. My father was then a director of a rubber company – they made various rubber parts for the motor car industry. His company had owned a subsidiary company, in Chichester, which had folded. The subsidiary company's factory needed to be sold. One way or another, my Dad had created the job of caretaker to this abandoned factory: someone who would be there to give a tour to prospective buyers, while making sure that no-one broke in or did damage. He offered that job to me.

At that time, I was trying to be a writer. Dad gave every sign of disapproving of such a course. He never mentioned then that he had once wanted to write himself, had actually sold his first story, and then never sold another thing, so that he abandoned the attempt, shut down the hope, and never admitted it, even when it might have been one thing we had in common. But, he said, I could write while I was in the factory. He could pay me a bit, and I lived cheaply in a pub, the Lamb, on East Street.

So I sat in the office, trying to be a writer, with a radio that played the Test match broadcasts. Every now and then I'd wander out on to the floor of the factory. It was the size of a large gymnasium, and it was nearly empty except for a few relics of the old rubber-goods business. There were formers on the floor, shapes that had once been dipped in latex – rows of hands for the making of rubber gloves and truncheon-like shapes that had produced condoms for bulls, necessary things in the insemination processes employed in bloodstock rearing. The hands and the ever-erect shapes made a surreal stage of the otherwise desolate factory.

One other thing remained: the company had made rubber balls, and there were hundreds of them around the place, like autumn leaves. For a would-be ball-player, this was an unexpected paradise. I had myself enacted some of Chelsea's best plays from the recent promotion season, hammering passes at the wall, meeting the return at glorious full stretch and lashing the ball into some 'goal'. When I grew bored with that, I measured out a 22-yard strip and bowled – I was Alec Bedser, Lindwall, Griffith, Lock and Trueman; I could imitate them all in the way some kids impersonate actors or rock singers.

A ball and a wall can last a lifetime. On a desert island, those are the luxuries I'd ask for, preferably an enclosure of walls, something like a large squash court where you can play the ball and calculate the return angles. All my life, I have loved to measure and scheme on the flight and bounce of a ball, its swing, its spin, its curves, and the possibility of meeting it precisely with the sweet spot of racket, bat, boot – or jock-strap.

I was playing like that — giving all too ample evidence of being a strange twenty-two-year-old — when Anne Power (who had worked at the now-defunct company as a secretary) came by with her two-year-old daughter, Kate. I think they watched me some time in wonder and amusement before they called out. We all fell in love. I hope the other parties won't quarrel with that: I know I fell in love with the two of them. Anne was not married, and Kate's father — who was more mysterious even than mine — was hardly referred to.

We got married that December which, in hindsight, was much too quick and impetuous. But it felt urgent and essential then, because we were in love, and were very happy. Everything in the world was light for our shining. And, for me, it is a vital part of the dark romance of the 1960s that one night in November, a cold night, Anne and I walked across Chichester to visit a friend, and discovered when we got there that President Kennedy had been shot in Dallas. It made us more in love, as if it was a way of taking deeper shelter in each other.

But that killing would shape my 1960s in other ways. The hot breath of American violence made me all the more fascinated by that country. The second shoe, two days later — Oswald offed on live TV — only made the would-be writer the more certain that the world was a *noir* story. And in only a few years, as someone in publishing, I would dine with Mark Lane — because Penguin published his *Rush to Judgment* — and feel that creeping mix of terror and excitement which told me our fathers and their generation had manipulated everything and were ready to screw the whole wide world. Everyone said when JFK was shot that everything had altered, and they were right enough. A whole skin of naiveté and hope was taken off by that acid. But the real change, for me, was when Oswald was shot. There was a large game out there that could be designed.

It is now getting on for 4:30 in the Wembley afternoon. The rain has moved on, but there seems no more chance of sun. The light is deeply overcast, and the clods of cut-up turf litter the pitch like droppings in a horse meadow. The fatigue in the players begins to confront an odd threat – that if no-one can be decisive now, they will have to play on for another half hour of extra time. There is an ominous air of every margin being cut fine. Make an error now and there is so little time left to recover.

'England don't get another one soon,' says my friend, 'they could get disheartened. Then they ease up, and, you see, the Germans could snatch one. Then we're on Queer Street.'

'We're more likely to score than they are,' I say. 'They know it.'

'Gives me the willies,' he says. 'Don't know why I bleeding come, really I don't.'

Tilkowski hesitates: is he nagged by the thought that he is always goal-kicking? He looks for a quick one-two with a defender so that he can throw, but England are covering, so Tilkowski sends out an accurate ball – a pass, really – to Schnellinger on the left. He takes it to the touch line, with Ball ready to challenge, and then passes on up past Held on the left. For a moment, chasing after it, Held has Cohen beaten for speed. But then Cohen reaches out with a tackle and puts the ball away for a corner.

As Held makes ready to take it, there is a dramatic pattern evident: England have ten men back in the penalty area – only Hurst has stayed up in attack; while Germany muster only four players in threatening positions. The corner is an out-swinger, and Peters beats Seeler to it in the air. His clearance falls to Beckenbauer, who takes a wild, first-time shot, sending the ball high and wide.

Banks taps the ball to Wilson, picks up the return and punts deep into the German half, where Weber heads the ball out to Overath, who passes it back to Schulz. He gives it to Haller, who plays it back to Schnellinger, but as the German defender moves forward Ball takes the ball from him and gives it to Hunt, who makes a deft, oblique pass on that is only just mis-timed for

Hurst. It is one more moment of desperate anticipation choked back – and one has known games where a hat-full of missed chances were eclipsed by an ugly goal at the other end.

Tilkowski rolls it out to Seeler, so natural a player he stirs one whenever he has the ball. Seeler gives it out to Emmerich on the left. He lays it back to Schnellinger and takes the return pass. He then crosses, to the level of around the eighteen-yard line. Jack Charlton easily heads away. Peters takes the ball on his chest, disdains Haller's presence and lobs a pass over his head to Bobby Charlton. Peters seems far more assured, as if stamina is coming to his aid. Bobby passes it on to Peters. He crosses the ball, and Schulz heads it away, to Beckenbauer, who is robbed by a raiding Cohen.

Cohen then gives a good pass to Bobby Charlton, who has the space and balance to deliver a long, but powerful shot. It hits a German defender and bounds away, but only to Wilson on the left. He crosses, deep to the far side of the goal, where Hurst seems to hold off Schulz as he jumps to head the ball down. Alas, there is no one there to use it, and the ball rolls across the face of the goal before Overath gathers it.

He passes the ball out to Held, on the right, for once, who gives it back to Haller and runs on for the return. Held has Moore covering him. He seems ready to cut across the field, but then he tries to beat Moore on the outside and sends in a fierce shot, which Banks watches go safely into the side-netting.

Banks clears to Wilson, whose pass forward is blocked by an unbalanced Schulz so that his clearance falls to Bobby Charlton, who gives it out to Hurst on the left wing. Hurst, a left-footed player, is able to get in a very good cross that finds Hunt with a split-second and half a yard. Hunt wheels to the right, but he is too slow or indecisive to finish. He bundles the ball leftwards and towards the goal, where Ball effectively urges Tilkowski and the ball over the goal line. It is a corner. It could have been a foul.

Bobby Charlton takes the corner, an out-swinger, and Tilkowski has one of his better punches to clear it out to Held. He gives to Haller, who nicely finds Emmerich clear on the left. He gives back to Held in the middle of the field. At first, Held beats Peters, by slipping to the right, but then he goes back to the left and Peters calmly steals the ball away. That tackle knocks the ball to Beckenbauer, who gives it out to Emmerich. But the ball comes to his right foot, and as he ponderously shifts to get it to his left, Ball takes it away with something close to contempt.

Ball gives to Stiles. It goes to Peters next, who finds Bobby Charlton on the left. His centre reaches Hunt, who makes a very good pass to Ball charging up on the right. Ball's shot is turned away at the near post by Tilkowski. Corner! How much longer?

17

So where was Alf Ramsey on November 22nd 1963, the day Kennedy was shot? In Ipswich, I presume, Dagenham or St Albans, or any of those suspiciously mundane English places? No, I don't mean to start rumours, or interrogate the man. He was very likely in his small office at the Football Association, assessing the pluses and minuses of the game England had played only two days before. I imagine him looking at the film, in the dark, on his own, running it backwards and forwards, scrutinising gesture and movement, like David Hemmings making a story out of the still pictures he stole in the park in *Blow-Up*. That's as close as Alf ever came to the grassy knoll – though he wouldn't have been wasted there, for he was the sort of man people don't notice.

At Wembley on November 20th, England had walloped Northern Ireland, 8–3. This was England's ninth game under Ramsey – nine games, that is, in twenty-one months, and it brought his record to:

P	W	D	L	GF	GA
9	6	1	2	32	16

Eight of those 32 goals, by the way, had been scored by Jimmy Greaves.

Not that Ramsey had begun well. His very first game, in 1963, against France in Paris, had been a 5–2 defeat, with this team:

                          Springett
          Armfield   Henry

      Moore   Labone   Flowers

  Connelly   Tambling   Smith   Greaves   B. Charlton

Of course, only two of that team, Moore and Bobby Charlton, would play in the July 30th test two-and-a-half years later. But seven of that first team remained in the 22-man squad named for the 1966 World Cup (the other five being Springett, Armfield, Flowers, Connelly, Greaves – all of whom, by 1966, counted as experienced, if not veteran, back-ups).

We should take that as a characteristic measure of the man's belief in loyalty and persistence. As England's sole selector, he was searching to find the best team. As we shall see, his mind stayed open surprisingly late. But he began as he meant to go on. He believed that there was a fundamental difference of class between good League-level players and those ready to play for England. And he believed in getting his defence set first, just like the old-time full-back. There's a telling statistic about Ramsey's administration, compared with that of his predecessor. Walter Winterbottom had to live with a selection committee that was swayed by local favourites, and every player who had a purple patch of a month or two, and then settled back to more mediocre League levels. Winterbottom managed England in 139 games, and in that time 78 players appeared for England three times or less; 35 of them played just once. Ramsey ruled for 113 matches, and only 42 men played three or less times. Of those, only 18 had just a single cap.

It's remarkable, too, how far Ramsey's selections were guided by matters beyond his control. I've said already that his World Cup side for 1966 could easily have had the benefit of left-back Roger Byrne; wing-halves Coleman and Edwards; and forwards Taylor and Pegg – all killed in the Munich crash. More than that, in April 1959, the Birmingham right-back Jeff Hall – who had been Byrne's partner in seventeen internationals – died of polio. Hall and Byrne together might have been too old by 1966, but surely they would have been a pair still in Ramsey's early years.

There were other decisive injuries: also in 1959, the twenty-year-old Alick Jeffrey, a phenomenally promising ball-player, suffered a career-ending leg fracture (incidentally, insurance paid him £4,000). Then in 1962, months before Ramsey came to power, Johnny Haynes, the skipper of England in 22 matches and the unquestioned on-field general, had a car accident that left him never the same player again. Haynes would have been only thirty-one on the day of the World Cup Final. He was England's most artistic, play-making forward around 1960; he was also rather slow, reluctant to defend and innately arrogant towards players who lacked his skills. Somehow one suspects that he and Ramsey wouldn't have got on. But Ramsey liked Johnny Byrne – more-or-less – the cocky, comedian-like inside-forward, who had moved from Crystal Palace to West Ham. Byrne was no Haynes, no Greaves; but he had something of both of them, and he was very familiar with Moore, Hurst and Peters. He played ten times for Ramsey's England, and scored 8 goals, before he damaged a knee so badly in the 1964 game with Scotland that he was slower afterwards. And then, in November 1965, after he had lost his England place, but when he was still a force, the centre-half Maurice Norman broke a leg badly.

One is always speculating over might-have-beens, and how twenty-year-olds would have developed. Still, England in 1966 might have fielded this team:

Banks

Shellito   R. Byrne

Coleman   Norman   Edwards

Jeffrey   J. Byrne   Taylor   Haynes   Pegg

And still no room for Greaves!

In Ramsey's second game, another defeat, at Wembley, to Scotland, he chose Banks in goal instead of Springett, who had had a bad game in Paris. Springett was elegant, polished and steady as a rule, but in the 1962 World Cup he had arguably failed with two of Brazil's goals in their crucial 3-1 victory. Once he failed to hold Garrincha's shot and Vava knocked in the rebound. It took no genius to see that Banks was, simply, a better goalkeeper. But Banks and Moore were the fundaments of Alf's defence.

Jimmy Armfield still dominated at right-back. He had been voted the best defensive player in the '62 World Cup. He was very popular, a natural leader and Ramsey's first skipper. But he was also a little past his best, and by June 1964 – when England beat Uruguay 2-1 at Wembley, a fine result – for the first time Ramsey put George Cohen and Ray Wilson together as full-backs. Thereafter, he never really changed his mind on them; they were set. The team for that Uruguay game was:

Banks

Cohen   Wilson

Milne   Norman   Moore

Paine   Greaves   J. Byrne   Eastham   B. Charlton

Incidentally, as Armfield was omitted – because he was injured in the first instance – so, for the first time, Bobby Moore was captain.

Liverpool's Gordon Milne – good in defence, thoughtful in attack – played 14 times for Ramsey. But Alf wasn't satisfied. He tried Flowers, Bailey of Charlton, and then Alan Mullery, who had just moved from Fulham to Spurs. In the summer of 1964, England went to Brazil to play in a mini-World Cup: it was a big step in the build-up and it was not a success. We beat the USA 10-0 on the way to Brazil, but then lost

5–1 to Brazil, 1–0 to Argentina, and got a 1–1 draw with Portugal. Ramsey saw that his defence was not right yet. Then, in April 1965, in what would be a 2–2 draw with Scotland at Wembley, he gave first caps to Nobby Stiles and Jack Charlton. Such moves added notable bite to the defence, not to say intimidation. Stiles, already, was known as a fierce tackler with a temper, while Jack Charlton was the hard centre in the altogether menacing Leeds half-back line of Bremner, Charlton and Hunter. But in the Scotland game, fifteen months before July 1966, Ramsey for the first time played the defence he would go for on the big day. Thereafter, he departed from it as seldom as possible. Banks-Cohen-Wilson-Stiles-Charlton-Moore had played together eight times before the first game of the World Cup – and then they played all six games of the competition itself. Ramsey's preparation began, and was most personal, in this notion that you begin by not being defeated.

Before Tilkowski can regain his feet, Ball runs after the ball that the keeper has turned away for a corner. Then, at a trot, he dribbles it back in an arc behind the press photographers to the corner flag. That extra nervous energy must daunt any German who bothers to watch it.

As Ball sets up the corner kick from the English right, there are ten Germans in their penalty area. The great entrance of the goal is guarded not only by Tilkowski, but by Höttges and Schnellinger standing on the goal-line. There are five Englishmen in the area, including Jack Charlton.

Ball stabs down on the kick so that the out-swinger has loft and back-spin. As it curls away, both Schulz and Weber go up for it, but neither of them is properly balanced to make a clearance. No English player jumps to contest the ball, and Weber's header drops at the feet of Hurst, about twenty yards away from the goal.

He has time to trap it, very correctly, and then as Seeler and Schulz converge on him, both from the right, he makes a small feint to the left that opens the gap between the two Germans.

Thus, as he moves back to his right, he is able to deliver a right-foot shot that threads the narrow space between them.

From that distance, it is not a dangerous shot. Indeed, it is going straight at Tilkowski. But the German full-back, Höttges, has come off the goal-line, and as he sees the shot approaching he reckons, instinctively, to kick it away. But the shot is fast, and he falls back as he swings at it.

The ball then leaps up in the air and to his left from his ill-timed contact. There must be wicked spin on the ball. But it is falling in front of a line of players – Hunt, Weber, Peters, Jack Charlton – as they advance on the goal.

They are about eight yards away from the goal. Tilkowski and Schnellinger are on the goal-line.

Jack Charlton will admit later hoping that the ball does not fall at *his* feet.

Then Peters strides forward, takes it on the volley, and drives the ball between Tilkowski and Schnellinger and into the net.

The netting behind them bulges with the force of the shot.

Peters is running, turning, ranting, screaming. Bobby Charlton tells Stiles, 'We've won!'

Gordon Banks runs to the half-way line to embrace Peters.

Tilkowski is tipped over on the goal-line, his legs in the air and wide apart like a busted V.

Twelve minutes to go.

2–1.

'How long?' asks my friend. 'How long to go?'

'A terrible time,' I say. 'They'd better get a third.'

18

Late in the second half of this Final match with West Germany, any objective spectator would have to subscribe to the notion that England were mounting a series of attacks in which Hurst, Hunt, Bobby Charlton, Ball and Peters all looked capable of scoring, with Cohen and Wilson overlapping and crossing, and with Moore, Stiles and even Jack Charlton all pressing forward. Though no advertised wingers were playing, several other players were from time to time filling the function of wingers. Indeed, the English team were interacting and exchanging roles in a way that fully exercised the German defence without baffling the English players themselves. Put that way, the performance of the team was as much a vindication for Alf Ramsey as the final result.

So it was all right on the day – even if the day took a long time dawning?

There's another way of describing what happened which turns on a Ramsey determined to have so solid a defence that the team could attack at will and – blessed with superior fitness and overwhelming crowd support – until the opponents cracked. When Ramsey named his 22-man squad for the World Cup Finals, its make-up indicated his leanings. Eleven of the men were goalkeepers or rear defenders. That is a way of saying that Springett, Bonetti, Armfield, Gerry Byrne (the Liverpool left-back), Flowers and Hunter never took the field in the final six games. Neither did George Eastham, the extra midfield player – he had been chosen, but ignored previously, in the 1962 World Cup.

So those men made up practice games and generally contributed to the morale of the party – and surely players like Springett, Armfield and Flowers (a trio with 125 caps) were equipped for that. Nor is there any reason to suggest that all 22 players should play: soccer had not then seen the virtues of platooning players to save energy and to exploit special situational skills. The lack of substitutes made the chosen 11 sacrosanct.

But then one has to concede that Ramsey's 22 had included three wingers – Paine, Callaghan and Connelly – who had effectively disproved their case by the quarter-finals. By the time of the match against Argentina, Ramsey had settled on his side, and one guesses that he had always meant to stick by it once that stage was reached. But that only indicated how unresolved he was about how, or even whether, his team should attack.

In late 1963, as Ramsey's England hit its string of six victories in a row, it had a fairly steady forward line:

Paine	Greaves	Smith	Eastham	B. Charlton

That was the line-up that beat the Rest of the World at Wembley in October, 2–1, in the Football Association Centenary match. Paine was playing well and scoring goals. Greaves and Smith, team-mates at Spurs, had a solid understanding. Eastham was creative, while Bobby Charlton roamed, yet still had the capacity to play the left wing. Smith, arguably, lacked the skills to play centre-forward at the highest levels, and he was past his prime. But Johnny Byrne was being groomed for that spot.

England's victory run was only broken – by Scotland, of course, at Hampden Park – in April 1964. Both Greaves and Smith were injured, and they were replaced by Hunt (in just his third international) and Byrne. Scotland won that game 1–0, and Bob Kelly of the Scottish FA was bold enough to tell the press that Ramsey's England were 'puppets. Ramsey pulls the strings and the players dance for him. I think he had theorised them out of the game.'

Long ago, in the days of Walter Winterbottom's 'leadership', Stanley Matthews had remarked on the cheek of managers telling the players how to play. Matthews had reckoned that you chose the team and then let the lads get on with it. That age was gone: managers now were figures – they had to do something. That didn't mean their heads were full of theory, or that their tongues were fluent. None of his players ever actually accused Ramsey of being a puppet-master on the field of play. But they were affected by his attitudes and his outlook. It was apparent that Alf was sometimes flummoxed by the mercurial play, and the impish personality, of both Greaves and Johnny Byrne.

Yet in May 1964, as a preparation for the trip to South America, England (with Byrne and Greaves prominent) had three fine victories. They beat Uruguay 2–1 at Wembley, both goals by Byrne. They went to Lisbon and beat the good Portugal team, 4–1, with a hat-trick by Byrne. And in the 3–1 defeat of the Republic of Ireland in Dublin, both Greaves and Byrne scored. The forward line now was:

Thompson/Paine	Greaves	Byrne	Eastham	Charlton

Then in three games in Brazil, that unit (or close to it) scored only two goals in two defeats and a draw.

Ramsey entered a period of experimentation in which, many felt, he abandoned class for long-shots. I think he feared Greaves and Byrne as a pair; he may even have seen their humour and high spirits as sources of trouble. (In New York, Ramsey had been horrified when a gang of players went on the town one night – and he was far from pleased with Bobby Moore, who was a pal to Greaves and Byrne, and not short on mischief himself.)

Still, in the next eighteen months, Ramsey tried Fred Pickering, Alan Hinton, Terry Venables, Frank Wignall, Barry Bridges, Mick Jones, Alan Peacock, Joe Baker and Gordon Harris, none of whom proved worthy of a place in the 22-man squad. There was one player coming to power whom a discerning manager might have tried: Peter Osgood, who was showing for Chelsea that one man might be both a striker and a ball artist. But Osgood, even when young, was famously insolent and cocksure. So often in English soccer, the really brilliant players – from Len Shackleton by way of Osgood, Rodney Marsh and Stan Bowles to Glen Hoddle – take on the reputation of being 'difficult' and not quite team players. But for Chelsea fans, it was outrageous nonsense to cap Bridges while denying Ossie.

And so, by early 1966, with the Final only months away, Ramsey was playing his given defence, along with a variety of forward lines that showed little purpose or policy. Indeed, it's likely that 'sure' picks like Bobby Charlton and even Greaves were beginning to be perplexed and disheartened by the changes. Hunt was in and out of the line-up: in 1964–5 he played five times in 21 matches. Alan Ball was first capped in May 1965, and it became clear that his energy, his work and his multi-positional flexibility all appealed to Ramsey. Of course, in those first months of 1966, the England team was without Greaves as he recovered from jaundice. Who knows, but for that we might not have seen Geoff Hurst, who played his first game for England as late as February 23rd 1966, ironically, against West Germany at Wembley. In April, he scored his first goal in the 4–3 defeat of Scotland at Hampden. And on May 4th 1966, against Yugoslavia, Hurst played with another new cap, Martin Peters.

Not that anything was clear or certain. Greaves returned for the Yugoslavia game and immediately began scoring goals. The forward line that day was:

Paine	Greaves	B. Charlton	Hurst	Tambling

In the next match, June 26th, against Finland, in a 3–0 win it was:

Callaghan	Hunt	B. Charlton	Hurst	Ball

Three days later, in a 6–1 victory over Norway, Greaves scored four times in this line-up:

| Paine | Greaves | B. Charlton | Hunt | Connelly |

On July 3rd, England beat Denmark 2–0 with:

| Ball | Greaves | Hurst | Eastham | Connelly |

And then, in the last game before the Finals themselves, Poland was beaten 1–0 with:

| Ball | Greaves | B. Charlton | Hunt | Peters |

In four of those games, Bobby Charlton had been effectively our centre-forward. Why not? And as a rule, he was playing with wingers, or wing-like players, and with Greaves, Hunt or Hurst close by. You can argue that Ramsey was keeping other teams off-balance, progressing so that no-one could be certain what team they would face. Equally, one could reason that the dour exponent of common sense was going by hunch and waiting for something to turn up. What is plain is that the system that worked on July 30th had not yet been put on the field.

And now, as never before, England begin to rampage at the German goal, or like kids wanting to get in on the act. From the kick-off, Overath holds the ball in the centre circle and then releases Schnellinger down the left. Plainly now, Schnellinger is moving urgently, but his attempt at a cross – or is it a shot? – cannons off Stiles's shoulder for a throw-in. Schnellinger takes this himself, and gives it to Overath. But the return pass is a set-up for England's off-side trap.

Stiles takes the free kick and sends it across-field to Banks, who throws out to Wilson. His pass finds Hurst playing deep, and he tucks it inside to Ball, who slips it outside to Peters. Peters is being harassed by Höttges when who should come racing up to him but Ball who, in effect, tackles Peters and canters on, pursued by Höttges. Schnellinger blocks Ball's way, but the left-winger for the moment draws the tackle, jinks left, and leaves Schnellinger on his back.

It is a sumptuous move which thrills the crowd, so that they have nothing but wrath when the pursuing Höttges dumps Ball in the corner of the field. As the free kick is set up, both Ball and Peters seem ready to take it, until Ball offers his special, stabbing thrust. The ball passes just over Hunt's head and nearly collides with the on-rushing Jack Charlton. The German defence is in disarray, and though the ball goes out to their left and is then briefly cleared, Stiles takes it from Held and puts in a cross to the left of the goal to Hunt and Ball, both of whom are found to be alone together and off-side. From the free kick, Tilkowski gives it to Haller, who falls into a promising forward exchange with Beckenbauer. But Haller's second pass to Beckenbauer is too much. Peters sees it coming and intercepts. He then passes the ball forward to Bobby Charlton, advancing down the inside left track. Bobby seems now eager for a moment of glory, and so from the corner of the penalty area, with Schulz closing in, he attempts a spectacular left-foot shot. But every spectator can see he's off-balance, and the ball winds away uselessly. No one begrudges this gesture: we would love to see Bobby triumphant at the end. Tilkowski rolls the goal-kick out to Schulz, who finds Seeler. He moves across-field, gives to Weber, and so to Overath. He passes back to Seeler, who now tries to move to the right. But the ball bounds into the English defence. When it springs back, Beckenbauer seizes it. But Moore easily gathers his lob, no matter that Stiles attempts and completely misses a bicycle shot at it. It's clear that the Germans have run out of plans for breaking down the English defence.

Moore's clearance goes to Schulz. He passes leftwards to Höttges, who gives it back to Schulz. As we have seen very rarely in this match, Schulz now carries the ball forward into the English half of the field. He crosses all the way over to the left wing, where Schnellinger comes crisply forward and delivers a powerful shot to the near post. But Banks is perfectly positioned and there is, for Germany, a chilling ease in the way he takes the shot.

The English clearance goes out down the right wing where, yet again, Ball, with an inside move, demolishes Schnellinger. Twice in a matter of moments, the blond back has been humbled by Ball's ferocious appetite and speed. He then gives the ball to Hurst – lying deep again, as if he has learned how to embarrass Schulz – who sends in a shot from outside the box. It beats everything, but yet again England's attack has made for a shot on goal.

Tilkowski's goal-kick is woefully mis-timed: the ball curls out of play no more than half-way towards the half-way line. Moore comes up to take the throw. He delivers it to Bobby Charlton, who tidily returns it. As Haller threatens Moore, the skipper gives it back to Wilson. In turn, he plays it back to Jack Charlton, and to a rising din of boos and derision the centre-half runs it all the way back to Banks. There are only moments to go, and possession play can use up the time. In years to come, that drab device would be cheered; a time would come when every irony deserted the cheers. But in 1966 the English fans loathed the nullity.

So Banks, to kill the boos, punts the ball away. Ball and Schnellinger go up for it together, without making solid contact. Weber clears. Jack Charlton knocks it back. Schnellinger boots it away. Then Cohen masters the ball, gives it to Ball – everywhere now – who gives it across-field to Hurst (deep again). He finds Peters moving up-field very rapidly and Peters sends in a powerful shot from just outside the penalty area. The crowd is chanting, 'We want three,' and they seem to have every chance of getting it.

Seven minutes to go.

19

It wasn't hard for fans to notice Ramsey's uncertainty; at his press conferences, he radiated uneasiness, and ranged from flat reiterations of the victory that was coming to wandering, obscure ruminations in which he (and his listeners) kept wondering if he was about to drop a grammatical clanger. It was just as easy for anyone to recognize that England weren't playing well or with flair. And the fans wanted everything: they yearned for victory, but they believed in 'artistic' soccer. Week by week, they saw it, at the club level. But week by week was a rhythm always denied to the national side.

Just because Britain had such a thriving League, its international performance suffered. Even in a World Cup year, club sides were often reluctant to release players for the full international preparation. And even in the year before July 30th – with extra matches to build cohesion – England played together only twelve times. There was no regularity; there was nothing like the familiarity of fans who 'knew' one another because they always stood in the same part of Anfield, Highbury or Stamford Bridge. There was always 'bloody Wembley', an unfeeling stadium, loathed by most fans, hard to get to, harder to enjoy, and so arranged that you felt miles from the players. Whereas, at the club level, fans love their stadium, its dingy setting, the bus and the walk to get there, the cramped closeness. God knows what might have happened to the English game if they'd played internationals at

Old Trafford, Anfield or even White Hart Lane. Imagine the Queen at White Hart Lane!

The run-up wasn't smooth. In October, England could only manage a goal-less draw against Wales at Ninian Park. Two and a half weeks later, at Wembley, they lost 3–2 to Austria – who weren't even qualifying for the World Cup! And then, on February 23rd 1966, the 1–0 victory over West Germany at Wembley (a Germany without Seeler, Haller or Schnellinger) was so tedious and leaden that it was greeted with derisive booing. In fact, Germany 'scored' an equalising goal, and had it disallowed, rather to the disappointment of a crowd that reckoned England deserved a harsher lesson.

That had been Geoff Hurst's first game for England, and Ramsey praised him afterwards because he ran himself silly. Yet many saw the stress on 'work' as a nearly penal condition that exposed the lack of skill or imagination. The lesson was horribly underlined two weeks later, when Manchester United went to Lisbon to play Benfica in the second leg of the European Cup quarter-finals. They went with a one-goal lead from the first leg, and they had every expectation of a struggle trying to hang on. Against Benfica, they were also playing something close to the Portugal side – and Portugal were already rated as a favoured team for the World Cup.

Something happened. Matt Busby urged his team to play tight and carefully at first – but he was talking to Bobby Charlton, George Best, Denis Law, Pat Crerand, Nobby Stiles, John Connelly. The game was live on television at home: 'everyone' was watching. United went crazy – in their very best lethal lovely way – and killed Benfica, 5–1. It was a rapturous evening, and it encouraged every fond thought that, at its best, the English club game was as good as anything in the world. One wonders whether Ramsey had the iron will to watch the whole game, or did he find a case for proving that the beauty was 'not relevant in this instance to England'. He didn't say that, but it was the way he dismissed arguments he couldn't handle. He had more reason to wait, for the brilliant but inconsistent United would be knocked out in the semi-finals by the lesser Partizan Belgrade.

Ten days later, a curiously English humiliation came from another quarter. The World Cup itself – the golden Jules Rimet trophy – was put on show in Westminster's Central Hall (a place famous for the annual Schoolboys' Exhibition) and managed to be stolen. Maybe it was Alf – in his Hitchcockian mode – just desperate to shift attention or bring in a little levity. There was one of those elaborate search operations that Scotland Yard is famous for. But then, a week later, a dog named Pickles found it in the front garden of a house in Norwood, wrapped in newspaper. Some rascal who had tried to hold up the world for £15,000 in ransom was eventually jailed. Pickles was a hero – he eclipsed even Chi Chi, the London Zoo panda, who was being sent to mate with An An in Moscow. Does it sound remotely plausible as a little bit of wicked free enterprise? I'd rather give credit to the glum Alf.

The Scotland game came a few days later, and then Alf was to name 40 players from whom the eventual 22 were supposed to come. This was a way of requiring that they keep in training once the regular season ended, and of warning their clubs that these men were likely to be needed. But it was also raw meat to the critics in the press.

The 40 included Peter Osgood, but not Johnny Byrne; Barry Bridges, but not Bobby Tambling. I mention that because in the Yugoslavia game a few weeks later who should be on the left wing but Tambling? Then, on May 6th, the 40 came down to 28. Osgood now was gone, but Tambling, Byrne and Brian Labone came back into favour. In fact, Labone was out as soon as he was in, because of injury. But the 27 left arrived on June 6th at Lilleshall Hall in Shropshire for the final two weeks of preparation.

Ramsey was in charge, with trainers Harold Shepherdson and Les Cocker and the team's doctor – another Ramsey innovation – Dr Alan Bass. Two weeks was probably as long as it could have lasted, even with armed guards. The country mansion had playing fields and facilities for many other sports. It had also a fence and gates. The players were not allowed out. Further, Ramsey made it clear that anyone escaping even to the local pub would no longer be among the 27 saved souls, but shipped home.

It was a twelve-hour day of intense physical training: naturally, young athletes were in good shape already, even if at the end of a season they had aches, injuries and bruises. But football then knew far less about preparing the body than, say, tennis and track athletics know now. Still, Ramsey and Cocker, especially, believed in hard regimes, in running, running, running. The endurance that England showed towards the end of full time and in extra time was laid down at Lilleshall. It may have been the largest part of Alf's theory – and it shows in the game in ways that by-pass skill. You can only be beautiful and effective if you are still standing up. In the Cup, the winning team would play six matches in twenty days: that is a tough task at any time, and Wembley's turf made it tougher still.

Above and beyond the running, the exercises and the soccer drills, the men could play badminton, tennis, basketball and even cricket in the afternoon. There were movies in the evenings. There were frequent medical inspections. The food was plentiful and fine, but unremarkable. And the 27 undoubtedly grew closer – there were several men in every bedroom – and became more possessed by a sense of purpose that might be unique in their lives. Ramsey was not intrusive, yet he watched the players for problems and grievances, and he was invariably in a track suit on the field with them. He was distant, yet not remote; and, if no-one loved him, he was widely respected – and feared. There were no favourites, not even Bobby Moore, and very few players were without some fear that they might be dropped when 27 became 22, or ignored thereafter. Among the attacking players, especially, there was no sound reason for anyone to feel secure – and thus extra motive to run that extra mile. If Alan Ball looked close to a great player in the final stages of the West

German match, it was because he had become a near world-class middle-distance runner.

On the last day at Lilleshall, Ramsey approached five players to tell them they were going no farther: Tambling, Johnny Byrne, Keith Newton, Peter Thompson and Gordon Milne. For Geoff Hurst, it was a strange feeling: at West Ham, he had grown up regarding himself as the professional work-horse and Johnny Byrne as the class act. But he was in and Byrne was out.

There was another sign: the 22 were now given numbers, and 1 to 11 looked suspiciously like the first team:

Banks

Cohen   Wilson

Stiles   J. Charlton   Moore

Ball   Greaves   B. Charlton   Hurst   Connelly

And so, the 22 set off for a short tour of the Scandinavian countries, to bring fitness to a perfect point of match play and to keep the team as an isolated unit as much as possible, cut off from the World, at which it was aimed. There would be games against Finland, Norway and Denmark, and then a visit to Poland, all within the space of ten days. All of which, fans followed from afar, understanding the morale-raising purposes of Lilleshall – for who had not heard of the Boy Scouts? – and scarcely estimating the rancour, say, of Jack Charlton or Nobby Stiles, cooped up together in an air of muscle liniment, sobriety and dogged paranoia.

For this fan, it was a rare time. My second daughter, Rachel, had been born the evening of the Yugoslavia game, so I can remember her slippery white arrival and have not the faintest memory of the game. There were three young children in the house by then, as well as two young parents. And we had to get domestic life settled down again and feeding brought to a sure rhythm, before the great crisis of the Finals.

Tilkowski puts the goal-kick square to his left to Schulz, who sends it on up that wing to Overath. His forward pass to Emmerich draws a foul tackle from Jack Charlton, which he protests out of ingrained habit or sense of injury. But Held's free kick, taken quickly, before Charlton can regain his position, floats over Seeler's head and goes out of play for a goal-kick. Banks now discovers a rare if timely uncertainty over which side of the goal to take his place kick from. The referee remarks on the oddity of this doubt. So Banks slides it out to Moore, who runs towards the touchline to control it, but just lets the ball cross the line. Weber throws it to Beckenbauer – every German move is urgent now, close to desperate; it is odd to see Beckenbauer hurried. He passes across to Held, who gives to Emmerich, takes a short return and is hustled off the ball by Stiles, who seems scornful of dainty inter-passing at this late stage.

Emmerich lines up to take the free kick. He has a very powerful shot, and he is taking a long run. But his kick proves to be a chip, elegantly judged for Weber in front of the goal. His header is awkward – he seems to wrench his neck – but he has a clear step of space and his header is not far wide.

Again, Banks has speed urged upon him by the referee. His big goal kick goes to Schulz, who masters it on the second effort and passes forward. As Schnellinger moves on to it, Moore comes in with a raised boot. It is a clear foul, despite a smattering of English boos to go with 'Rule Britannia'.

Schulz taps the free kick to Beckenbauer, who works a wall pass with Haller and is only half-set for a long shot that Stiles deflects away for a corner. Beckenbauer himself hurries to take this corner, but it is a poor effort that Moore first controls, then dribbles into the corner, and finally dispatches to Peters. This is a typically cool extrication, but Moore is not really harassed by any of the Germans.

Peters gives it to Ball, who shakes off Höttges's tackle, and then sends a deep, reverse ball across his body that frees Hunt in a very menacing position. It is a killer pass, thirty yards or so, splitting the defence. And Hunt has Bobby Charlton and Hurst with him, spread across the field. But he makes his pass too square and too quickly: so Schulz can stay with Bobby and trap him as the ball gets to him. A man with more finishing instinct than Hunt possesses might have gone all the way to goal himself, drawing the defender, and then freeing Bobby.

Tilkowski sends the goal-kick to Overath, and then it goes by way of Schulz and Emmerich towards Schnellinger. But Jack Charlton takes the ball on his chest and boots it away – to Weber. He gives it to Schnellinger, who passes to Emmerich, who at last gets in a long shot. But Banks handles it with absolute ease.

He sends it wide on the right to Ball, who is shifting all the way across the field in move after move. He feeds Hurst around midfield – Hurst has seemingly elected to play at that depth now. He moves forward with the ball, and from nearly thirty yards puts in a woeful shot that curves away towards the corner flag. Such a shot is a pass to the opponent. A more experienced Hurst would surely hesitate, pass back, and set up a circle of possession.

One more German goal-kick – how many more can there be? – goes to Weber, to Overath, back to Weber and to Beckenbauer. He passes forward to Schnellinger, blatantly an attacker now, and Moore challenges him in a way that leaves no room for doubt. The push is called. Beckenbauer takes the free kick and passes to Overath. He gives to Weber, and so to Schnellinger and Haller, who crosses the ball. But England clear it away: Ball seizes on the loose ball, gives to Moore, and the skipper passes it out to Hurst on the half-way line.

He gives it to Bobby Charlton, who sends it square, to the right to Hunt, who circles round to his right with the ball and gives it back to Bobby, who is tackled by Schulz. He clears it to Schnellinger, who feeds Haller. He passes to Seeler, who sends a crossfield ball to Overath. Overath manages to slip the tackle by Peters and takes a long shot that skids across the English goal and goes a couple of yards wide.

There are two minutes to go.

'Take your time, Gordon,' says my friend, as Banks sets up the goal-kick. 'Don't kick till you see the whites of their eyes.' The sun is fighting to come out again, as if it wants to be here for the victory. 'As long as no-one does anything stupid,' my friend is saying to himself.

20

Returned from Poland, the England party moved into the Hendon Hall Hotel, their final base for the climax to the campaign. The short tour of Northern Europe had been a tremendous boost to confidence: four matches played, four victories, twelve goals scored and one against. (A sceptic might have added that four goals came from Greaves against a weak Norway, while four were added by defenders – but Hurst, Ball and Bobby Charlton hadn't scored.) The English players believed in themselves. Ramsey was steadfast with his story that they would win. The bookmakers made them favourites – West Germany were actually 20 to 1.

And so the Cup began on the evening of Monday July 11th at Wembley as England played Uruguay. Ramsey did not quite pick his 'first 11': Geoff Hurst had not been impressive on the tour, so Alf took his usual defence and put Ball, Greaves, Bobby Charlton, Hunt and Connolly in front of them. The Queen was there for the opening ceremonies; there were the flags of all the nations; everyone hoped for a set-piece, as well as an England victory.

The 0–0 draw that followed was a dire spectacle, with the Uruguayans totally committed to defence and negativity. But it was also proof that that sort of system, allied to the greater ball skills displayed by many of the South Americans – Troche and Rocha, in particular – was still enough to confound England, to leave them looking frantic, overly masculine and clumsy. The

Uruguay team was far better than the method their manager, Ondino Viera, employed. Their goalkeeper, Mazurkiewicz, was not far from the level of Banks. Cortés was always dangerous. And even for a packed nine-man defence, Uruguay could muster startlingly rapid raids. Had they been charged with more daring and more faith in attack, England might have had a harder time still.

As it was, England dominated: they forced 16 corners to 1 for Uruguay. But they retaliated to harsh tackles. Stiles threw a punch and was lucky to stay on the pitch. Hunt was inept, Bobby Charlton aimless, and Greaves at a loss. All of a sudden, this England looked like a team that had not yet worked out how to play the modern game. It was a blessing that Uruguay had failed to obtain the release of several players who were involved in the Argentinian League.

'We can still win it,' Alf told the press, and he was very big on not conceding a goal. He had a theory that England could even qualify from their group with three goal-less draws.

But he guessed the team was tense. On the Tuesday, he took everyone down to Pinewood Studios. *You Only Live Twice*, the next James Bond picture, was being shot there. So the lads gawped at Sean Connery. They met Britt Ekland and Norman Wisdom. They got to sip at champagne. And Alf gave a little thank-you speech – 'I'd just like to thank Seen Connery for giving up his time' – that had most of the players giggling. Alf liked movies. He knew it was Sean. But he got tongue-tied and fussy.

At their hotel, watching other games, England were impressed by West Germany's 5–0 execution of Switzerland, with two goals scored by Beckenbauer. It made goal-less draws seem less comforting. They also saw Hungary beat Brazil, 3–1, after the Brazilians had elected to rest Pelé for the game.

On the following Saturday at Wembley, England faced Mexico. Alf dropped Ball and Connelly and replaced them with Paine and Peters. There was still no Hurst. The Mexicans shared the Uruguayan attitude but none of their skills: this was one of the weakest sides in the tournament. But still, England struggled against the packed defence. They had all the play, but Paine was hurt, and the English attack seemed very disjointed. But then, after thirty-five minutes, Bobby Charlton gathered the ball, carried it deep into the Mexican half, with defenders falling back, and at last unleashed an immense twenty-five-yard shot with his right foot. An awesome goal, that crushed Mexico. Yet all England could add was one more goal by Roger Hunt, who snapped up a muffed clearance by the keeper.

The following Wednesday evening, England had the formality of a third group game with France, who had only drawn with Mexico and lost to Uruguay. Ramsey now replaced Paine with Ian Callaghan. Ball and Hurst were still omitted. However, there was a surprise: with nothing to lose, France attacked, and controlled long sections of the game. If two of their players had not been injured, they might have come much closer – and one of those players, Simon, was hurt in a horrible, illegal tackle by Stiles that could have had him sent off. After the game, there would be protests from other countries and calls for Stiles to be banned. But Ramsey stuck by his player and even identified with him. Hunt scored twice for England, once when clearly off-side and once when Simon was flat out on the ground. But England were wretched again, perpetually falling for the French off-side trap. In an odd way, a jittery England gathered themselves afterwards around Ramsey's defence of Stiles: after all, this was a team effort, and Nobby was one of them – even if he had acted out the worst traits in English football according to the rest of the world. England had five points. They had shown their limits with ghastly clarity. But they were united. And the question was clearer now: was there a team in the Cup good enough to beat them? For Brazil had failed to qualify.

On the Saturday, July 23rd, England would meet Argentina in the quarter-finals. Argentina had qualified with nearly England's record: five points and four goals; they had held West Germany to a goal-less draw. They were along the lines of Uruguay: a very disciplined defensive team that also possessed remarkable players – their captain Rattín and Onega in mid-field; and Artime and Mas as strikers. So much depended on their attitude. Had they learned enough from England's three games to see that creative attack might carry the day? Or would defensiveness provoke the English readiness for force?

Ramsey thought hard, and decided to give up on wingers: Paine, Connelly and Callaghan had done too little to justify the system. Instead, he now settled on what would be *the* team, though surely he was ready to change it again if he felt pressed. Ball and Peters would play. Greaves was gone – he had hurt his shin against France, that was the excuse. And Hurst would play.

That Saturday's game was the ugliest and most melodramatic of the tournament. It was widely hailed as a travesty and a disgrace, and it is not too much to say that it was remembered, on both sides, in what would be, in 1982, an absurd but tragic war fought over the Falkland Islands. Let us say that two elaborate, and unduly armed, sets of prejudices collided.

In England, it was reckoned that Latin Americans played their own dirty, but sneaky, kind of football. They did not enjoy brutal physical challenge – the honest English way. But they kicked players off the ball; they held shirts, or flesh; they nagged, impeded; they might spit; they faked injuries and acted up a storm with referees. For their part, the Argentinians believed that England was a colonial relic (much involved, and greatly to British profit, in Argentina), a model of stupid arrogance, and – as footballers – violent, impulsive and fearless. We are regularly taught that prejudices are errors. But just as often we know that practice is controlled by perceptions. England and Argentina knew they were right. Both sides entered the match ready for trouble, and with a plan for dealing with it.

The game quickly became chaotic, in part because of the helpless efforts of the German referee, Herr Kreitlein, to control it. Both sides were ready to foul: it is still the English wisdom that Argentina was the chief offender, though a letter from Lord

Lovat to *The Times* a few days later pointed out that there were only nineteen fouls by Argentina and 33 by England. Most people saw Stiles strike the first blow – it was by now nearly a duty for him to do so. The Argentinians responded in kind. But what was more significant was the way Rattín, their skipper, a very tall, handsome midfield master, began to hound Kreitlein with questions, abuse and palpable, sneering outrage. Meanwhile, Kreitlein was taking names like a police sergeant who had never heard of official programmes.

The climax of the match came after thirty-seven minutes. Rattín had been booked for one foul. Then he committed another. The referee did nothing. Rattín went into more complaints. And then Kreitlein ordered him off the field, as he admitted later, not so much for what was said (the referee had no Spanish) as for the unmistakable contempt with which it was offered. Rattín protested. He lingered for maybe ten more minutes. The game came to a halt. Other officials were on the side-line trying to restore order. At last, Rattín departed.

The fouling went on. Argentina played with ten men, and on several occasions they out-classed England, especially when Onega had the ball. You can say that Argentina was paranoid, that they pre-empted robustness with violence. You can also wonder if England didn't succeed by dragging the game down to their own, reduced level of skill. If Argentina had played soccer such as they were capable of, there's no solid reason for thinking England would have survived.

Still, with twelve minutes to go, Peters, out on the left, sent in a cross. Hurst, running into empty space, rose, twisted his body and let the ball hit his forehead, from where it had nowhere to go but into the goal. That was it: 1–0, England were through and Ramsey, in the dressing-room, was saying that the Argentinians had behaved like animals.

Soccer deserved better, and it got it the following Tuesday when England played Portugal in the semi-final. This was maybe the best exhibition of competitive, creative football in the tournament. The game was hard and clean, and it was distinguished by the Portuguese habit of congratulating opponents for particularly fine bits of play. Stiles rose above himself, largely because he was charged with marking the Portuguese genius, Eusébio – a task he had already performed for Manchester United in its two European Cup games with Benfica.

The English alignment, held over from the Argentina match, clicked for the first time. Bobby Charlton had a superb game. He scored both English goals – the first, with delicate coolness in a scene of grand confusion, the second with a fulminating shot. Banks made great saves. Portugal got a late goal – a penalty – and then attacked for ten minutes seeking an equaliser. But England held out. And for the first time, they had played very well.

In that last passage against Portugal, England played as if in an ordeal, that of losing something briefly possessed. There is no crisis quite as neurotic as the one that waits for the last whistle. It is as fatalistic as a fighter who knows he may be killed before he hears the final bell. And that foreboding can be rewarded.

It will be now as, for the second time in a row, England deliver themselves of a good game.

Banks runs to take the goal-kick: surely there is no law that says he must run; but he has been pained by Dienst's accusation that he might be wasting time. So he kicks it away and the ball goes over the half-way line, where Höttges twists his body to head it back.

The ball arcs forward, and there is Peters jumping to head it away. Slower than ever, the ball climbs and falls and Beckenbauer, beating Bobby Charlton, heads it back again.

This header bounces, as it goes towards Held. This is important, for the bounce would not have carried over Held's head. But Jack Charlton, recklessly, leans over Held to head the ball away. Later, the English will argue that Held backed into Jack. Not so. He may never have known the Englishman was there. But without need or reason, Charlton has fouled.

He disputes the referee's call. Stiles adds complaint in that gutter-snipe way he has. But Herr Dienst has no doubt. As Emmerich lines the kick up – thirty-five yards out, to the left of the goal – the referee marches the ragged, disobedient wall back to something closer to its proper distance.

Emmerich takes the kick. It is gentle. It slides past the wall. Ball falls as he reaches to stop it.

The ball goes free to Held. He shoots at goal.

But the ball instead strikes Schnellinger on the arm, without any intent at foul.

It might have bounced away anywhere. That German team could be there still thirty years later, practising the play, and they would not once more have had it fall, as it does, from Schnellinger's helpless arm, down and across, between Seeler and Wilson, so that it comes to Weber, who lunges out his right leg and tucks it into the goal.

From out of the muddled blue, disaster.

2–2.

England kick off. Bobby Charlton gives it to Hurst, who passes back to Jack Charlton. But before the ball reaches him, the referee has blown the first of three blasts signalling full time. Jack hurls his bitter hands in the direction of Herr Dienst, so woeful, so cursed, at having committed that needless foul.

There will be more.

'Is this a game or what?' says my friend. 'And we're here.'

'You know,' I say, 'there was a World Series game – '

'What's that?'

'Baseball.'

'Oh, yeah?'

'And it went into extra time. Extra innings they call it. It was one of those back-and-forth games, with changes in the lead.'

'I know.'

'And a batter comes up, and he turns to the catcher, and he says, "Can you *believe* this game?"'

'Oh yeah? That's nice. When was that?'

'Oh,' I say, fumbling a little, but too happy with magic to lie, '1975.'

He looks at me, my friend. He has guessed all along that I am not quite the real thing. But now he wonders if it is simply a matter of my madness or his being my prisoner.

FULL TIME

I cannot help but wonder how Herr Dienst elected to blow for full time just a second or so after England had taken the kick-off following Weber's equalising goal. That would seem to mean that the referee reckoned there were just a couple of seconds left to play when Weber scored. But then suppose – if Weber's shot had hit the post and bounced out to Höttges, if Höttges had taken the ball to the by-line and then crossed it to the far post, if Held had headed it back, and if that spinning, twisting ball had fallen just where Jack Charlton reckoned to boot it, but the ball spun and caught only the edge of his vicious foot, and then hit Weber's unsuspecting, entirely innocent knee, so that it trickled into the goal past a dumbfounded Banks – is *that* a goal? Or does it come more than two seconds after 'full time'?

This is not to challenge Herr Dienst's integrity, much less the fine running of his watch – surely, in this case, a Swiss watch? But time in football is a remarkable thing – precise, yet malleable and elusive – and it is my opinion that the inmost nature of any sport bears upon the way it employs time.

Football matches are played in two halves of forty-five minutes each. As the ball is first touched at the opening kick-off the referee is required to start his watch. By implication, therefore, most referees would seem to wear or carry a stop-watch, or a watch that has a stopping, and aggregating, function. The referee is the sole time-keeper. In those stadia where a clock is in evidence, that clock has no part in the officiating of the game – for that very reason, I suspect, few football grounds have clocks.

But the referee does not meekly wait for the forty-five minutes to elapse, or for something like an alarm clock to go off in his pocket. He is charged by the rules of the game to add on something extra, at the end of forty-five minutes, to compensate for time lost to injuries and other stoppages. All of which assumes that he does have a watch he can stop – or that he has a second watch on which he can keep a count of undue stoppages.

There had been an injury to Tilkowski in this game, a moment when the German trainer had been signalled on to the pitch to apply restoratives and comfort to the German goalkeeper. Thus there was a period of time in that first half when play 'stopped'. In the quarter-final match with Argentina, proceedings were substantially interrupted by the events that followed the referee's decision to have Antonio Rattín leave the game. Some observers reckoned the fuss took as much as ten minutes. There was a Cup Final once where the ball burst, and there have been games here and there where the crowd broke on to the field and prevented play for several minutes.

But play stops and starts all the time. In any given half of football, the ball will go out of play – it is even known then as a 'dead ball' – between thirty and seventy times. It goes out of touch; it is retrieved by ball-boys or thrown back out of the crowd; it is tested by the thrower and then given to another player to throw in – anything from three to twenty seconds elapses on a throw-in. Then there are goal-kicks, where the keeper has to recover the ball, make a firm flat spot from which to kick it . . . and even be warned by the referee for time-wasting. Then there are fouls where, perhaps, an offending player has to be told off, and where the defensive wall has to be nagged into being ten paces away from the ball. Take it all into consideration, and it is likely that in any forty-five minutes of 'continuous' soccer, the ball is dead for at least ten minutes. In the first half of this game today, for instance, the ball was dead fifty-nine times.

Of course, those five minutes are a continuation in one respect: they allow players to regain their proper position. Indeed, for many players those ten minutes are as active and demanding as any others. Yet one has known teams that also employed the touchline for purposes of rest and recuperation, and a lot of fouls are committed simply because a defensive alignment needs to regather. But those stoppages are not accounted for in the game's time. Rather, there is the notion that forty-five minutes is forty-five minutes, and that each game develops a rhythm of its own.

Living in England, watching football, I seldom noticed those points. The referees were frequently held to be blind, stupid and even prejudiced in the observation of ordinary fouls, but no-one really disputed their time-keeping. Of course, towards the end of a close game, the light failing, and Chelsea hanging on to a 2–1 lead, the fans would start to whistle themselves. But they were urging on the referee. Their anxiety was ironic and amused. No one could *see* the referee's watch, or reliably remember the stoppages that might incur 'extra' time. The whistle was, and is, trusted. In a Cup replay, if the score was tied after full time, there would be two 15-minute halves of extra time. If the score was still tied, there would be a second replay on another day. And, if necessary, another replay.

My thoughts took another direction when I came to live in America. Perforce, at the age of thirty-five or so, if I wanted a sporting life, I had to learn three games that – in 1975 at least – were scarcely known, let alone understood, in Britain: American football, baseball, and basketball. In two of those sports, there is an official clock; and in the third there is a superb, haunting state of timelessness – that only serves to make time a paradigm of its role in real life.

At the same time, in America, I became increasingly perplexed that soccer – truly, the world's game – could not take hold as a national American pastime. Why? I wondered. One obvious answer was that the continuous line of play in soccer allowed no room for commercial breaks in the television coverage that is part of the structure of American sports. In the late 1970s, in the USA, there was nearly a successful soccer league – it had Pelé, Chinaglia, Beckenbauer and many other great players striving to establish it. There were good crowds at the games – and soccer was and is played a lot at American schools, where parents justifiably fear the physical damage of American football. But, on television, the games were interrupted, broken away from, and the line was never the same again. In narrating this great match, I have generally used goal-kicks as breakers, and in a book, I hope, that can work. But 'live' coverage cannot endure going away. My passages are passages from legend: you and I know that I am describing, or re-enacting, a known and given event. We are celebrating a certain 'once upon a time', whereas to watch a soccer match live is to experience, to pass, present time.

Still, I was fascinated by the performance of American football and basketball in which the several referees, umpires, judges and linesmen are not responsible for timekeeping. There is a time-keeper and a clock – or rather several versions of the one inescapable, electronic measure of time – that everyone in the arena can see. And in both those games, 'dead' balls stop the clock. If a ball goes out of play, no time elapses. When a player takes free throws in basketball, the clock freezes. In American football, as players huddle before a play, the game clock is still; it starts only when the ball is snapped. (There is a subsidiary clock that counts down the allotted time for a huddle, but that time is not part of the game's time.)

In addition, both games have 'time-outs', occasions when one side or the other (or even the television network) can signal for time, and there is a stoppage in which plans are made and players substituted. Each side has three time-outs in a half in football, but there is also a two-minute warning stoppage – two minutes before full time – and there are official time-outs to move the chains that measure attacking progress.

This means that an American football game with four fifteen-minute quarters can last three or three-and-a-half hours in 'real' time. At first, the foreign spectator will be confused by the broken structure, and bored by the delays, but then he will come to see the immense strategic role of time. American football is a kind of military board game with human counters, but it is an exquisite play upon time. And in basketball, as in American football, a great game, a finely contested match, invariably hinges on the expert use and control of seconds in the last few minutes. These are games where the coaches are therefore vital, and they are seen on television, on the sidelines – sometimes equipped like generals with clipboards and walkie-talkie sets – estimating not just space, talent, motion and plan, but the inexorable passage of time. These men are like immensely energetic, greedy capitalists cramming as much as they can into the last split-second of life.

When basketball and American football are at their best, the last quarter of the game, or the last quarter of the last quarter, becomes prolonged, microscopically detailed. So much happens at every click of the clock, the game needs slow-motion television replay for its fullest appreciation. And so there are sports in which, while it is one thing, and one hugely exciting thing, to be *there*, still the connoisseur's gaze is on television where there is a way to re-examine the fragments. But such games, sooner or later, will turn on whether Joe Montana can get one last pass off, and whether Jerry Rice can catch it. Or, to be more infinitesimal still, it is a matter of the clock standing at 00.02 as Larry Bird makes to throw, 00.01 as the ball leaves his hands, then 00.00 and the damning buzzer with the ball still in the air, and beyond that with the swish of nothing but net. That is a score, that can be the game, for time was still running when Bird made the shot. And Bird's mind was calibrated as closely as that.

Then there is uproar, and grown men are declaring that this was the greatest game they ever saw – grown men are maybe the only living creatures who can say that so often, so regularly.

Then there is baseball, which could go on for ever. The game begins at 1.05 or 7.35 p.m., and after that there is the weather or local night curfew laws to contend with. The two sides will have nine innings each in regular time. If they are tied after that, they play extra innings – until there is a winner. There are no drawn or tied games in baseball. Indeed, American sport does all it can to avoid a draw or a tie. Cricket can be played to an exact tie, but only because it has no provision for extra innings. Baseball games have gone to twenty and thirty innings, and into the next day after a suspension in the name of night. But there is no clock, and no one innings or at-bat that might not, in theory, go on for ever – or be extinguished in one swing of the bat.

I was very lucky in that, about six weeks after I had first gone to live in America, baseball arranged to offer what veterans agree is one of its greatest games ever. This was Game 6 of the 1975 World Series, the Boston Red Sox v. the Cincinnati Reds. I had gone to teach in New Hampshire, and I had been taken by friends to see a few games at the close of the Red Sox season, at Fenway Park, the loveliest sports ground I have ever known.

I was not there for Game 6. Rather, I watched in the large, beautiful, lake-side house my family and I were renting in rural New Hampshire. Not that the family was doing well. Not that I was behaving well, or kindly, or even decently. Not that parts of me didn't long to be back 'home' even as I realised that my grasp on that home was slipping.

The turmoil was such that the game was especially welcome: great games, it seems to me, come to the aid of hard times, like good movies. So I was alone in the living-room with the television set, watching a game for which I had as yet a very incomplete understanding. But I loved the Red Sox already, and I wanted them to win. In fact, at that point, Cincinnati led the Series, 3–2. Game 6 could decide the best-of-7 Series.

Game 6 had been delayed several days by rain: this was late October when you can feel the long winter coming, like war, in New England. Boston took an early lead: the graceful Fred Lynn homered. The Red Sox pitcher, Luis Tiant, began majestically.

But the Reds caught up to him. By the middle of the eighth inning, the Reds led 6–3.

But in the bottom half of that inning, the Boston half, the Sox got two men on base. Then a pinch-hitter, Bernie Carbo, came up. Last chance? Carbo looked awful and slow. Maybe he despaired of being skilful, or talented. So he swung. And he hit a home run. 6–6. The ninth inning came and went, and the game was tied still. With every inning now, the tension mounted. It was in the tenth that Pete Rose of the Reds came up to bat, turned to the Boston catcher, Carlton Fisk, and – so much in awe of this living theatre – asked, 'Can you *believe* this game?'

To take life to that pitch – when all is really absurd or meaningless – but to do it so that people whose family life is ending forget it for a moment. And to be in a game that will be honoured when all its players are dead. A few times in my life I've felt that exhilaration.

The game went on. It was past midnight. In the bottom of the twelfth, Fisk came up to bat – a New Hampshire native, a superb-looking man, a master of his own act – and he hit a ball just inside the foul post into the net above Fenway's green wall. Home run. 7–6, Red Sox. We would go to Game 7 – if winter didn't set in first.

The Red Sox lost Game 7. The Red Sox have not won the World Series since 1918, after which they sold Babe Ruth to the damned Yankees and settled into a curse that may outlast us all.

So there is time big and time small. And I only wish to observe that at or around 4.40 p.m., Greenwich Mean Time, on July 30th 1966, referee Gunther Dienst *chose* when it was full time. As if to say, after West Germany had equalised, well, yes, that feels like the proper close to a chapter. There was that much of the author in him.

EXTRA-TIME

21

Last night was New Year's Eve, and my wife and I watched *Schindler's List* on videotape. As we talked about the picture, I wondered what it said about me, knowing that the next day, today, I would begin to write about extra time, in many ways the most urgently felt battle with Germany I have known. For I cannot claim that I understood, or was enlisted in, the four-and-a-quarter years of World War Two that overlapped with my life. It was all I knew – and nothing that I understood. That came later, as I saw and asked about what must, for 1945, have been rather decorous, very restrained, newspaper photographs of men in pyjamas – or so it seemed – the survivors found in concentration camps.

There were two Jewish households on our street in those years, and the years afterwards: one Dutch and wealthy; the other German maybe, or Austrian, and lower-class. My Dad made jokes about the latter, about their being Jewish, about their dirtiness, their strangeness. These were not friendly or good jokes, and they were not made to these people's faces. The Dutch family he honoured, and ignored; their Jewishness was not mentioned. Nor, it seems to me, in retrospect, was that attitude uncommon. There was a lot of 'ordinary' anti-Semitism in my childhood London, and no sense that the war was being fought over the fate of the Jews.

What I'm trying to say is that, if the Germans had taken England in 1940 or 1941, I suspect that many people would have watched the working-class Jews being removed. They would have had no real doubts about where they were going, and they would have been horrified. But many people would have complied. They might have helped the wealthy Jews. So much of England's functioning is to do with class. The English, though, would have bowed to Fascism's power, no matter what Churchill urged upon us. There would have been resistance, of course, even one of the more sardonic, humorous and inventive resistance movements. For the English hate and scorn foreigners – rather more than most races do. But the English would have done what the generality of Germans did – they'd have accepted their own fear, and fear's prod, that power. We would have behaved less than well, and lied later when our memories were re-directed.

In other words, I cannot believe that Germans are 'worse' than us. On the other hand, I am fifty-four and I have never been in Germany beyond the act of changing planes in Frankfurt. I don't really want to go there, and that is only because of some irrational influence left over less from war itself than from the stories told about war. Throughout my youth, there was a constant portrayal of German cruelty in movies, books, radio, and general talk. I resent the influence it had on me, and I know that I should be wise and adventurous enough to go and live in Germany. But then I see *Schindler's List* – a film for which I have mixed feelings – and everything comes back in the English actor's portrait of the terrible German camp commander.

More than fifty years after the war, and even in the age of the Channel Tunnel, I see and feel a Britain that is still disdainful of Europe, rigorously superior to foreigners, and anti-German. Britain still has the most confused feelings about being in Europe. In extra time, this Saturday at Wembley, a cry began to be heard – sudden, inexplicable roars of, 'Eng-*land*, Eng-*land*', with a thousand or so voices in perfect unison. How do crowds learn or know how to do that? Are they led or directed? Or is there some force in crowds that waits to be tapped by rare crisis? The two syllables of 'Eng-*land*' were not sung or chanted, but barked out, like blows – it was like punching the idea of an enemy. Perhaps, in a way, it was even a little Germanic – and surely one reason the English fear and loathe the Germans is out of a sense of likeness and special rivalry.

In the game itself, in regulation time, I think the fact that the opponent was West Germany was taken as a mere coincidence, even what the English sometimes regard as irony. It was not felt or registered as part of the old hostility. But with extra time, with the exhaustion, the severity and the extremism that came with it, the crisis took on epic and mythic undertones. It was beyond a joke, past irony; these were Germans, and you have to kill Germans to beat them, don't you? I know that mood was there as the shadows lengthened and the game became more open and deadly because of fatigue.

So I want to stress something else: that a game, a piece of sport, is valuable because it is unnecessary, unimportant, not just trivial but weightless. And because a game is all of those things, it can reach a profundity that the solemn events will never claim. A game can always be read as a metaphor for deeper conflicts, antagonism and violence – a game is a prelude to war, in that sense. But a game, or play, is also a way of passing time when time is all we have; it is an urge towards movement, action and maybe even grace as opposed to being stagnant and inert. And winning doesn't matter, because victory is always an illusion. All these players will pass and be forgotten, even the great ones. I know, I know, I make heroes of them because I long for that not to be so: I would want to beat death. I want to win. But I know we all lose. And I know that every football game between England and West Germany is like the games that were played on Christmas Day, 1914 – the first Christmas of trench warfare – as two armies came up out of the ground and kicked a ball around in the snow.

In other words, I have never felt better about Germany than that day in July 1966. The feeling isn't resolved; I know; it never will be; or not for centuries. And it is a great contradiction to want to win so much while knowing that everyone loses. Very well, I contradict myself – a phrase I read first, I think, in Norman Mailer's *Advertisements for Myself*, another powerful influence in those years. Mailer got the line from Walt Whitman, but Mailer seemed to me to be an ideal endless midfield worker, making extravagant connections, and running, running, running.

The players were appalled to think of another half an hour. Some fell over, some sat on the ground. Others felt they had to keep moving: for rest might betray them. Then Ramsey strode on to the pitch. He was wearing a track-suit top – and regular shoes. As if boots would have been a touch common. He gathered the team in a circle around him – only Bobby Moore remained sitting on the grass – and he told them, 'You've beaten them once and then lost it. Now beat them again.' Then he asked them to look at the Germans, who were some of them flat out, and he said, 'Look at them, they're finished'. He didn't read them the riot act, or sing patriotic songs. He just told them to do it again, and in the way he put it he told them the only important thing – that they were stronger, fitter, and natural winners.

And so the players make ready again. The red shirts of England are darker now from sweat. Some of the players, Stiles and Ball, let their socks slip down to their ankles. Those garters can help bring on cramp attacks. And just stopping running now can cool the muscles so that they lock.

The Germans kick off: Overath, Held and Seeler are in the centre circle, muttering, too weary to make a plan. This will be instinctive soccer.

From the kick-off, Overath swings it left and forward to Emmerich. He glides past Cohen with the ball, but as Stiles approaches, the German kicks away and the ball bounces off Stiles and out of play.

Schnellinger takes the throw-in and Emmerich heads it back to him. Whereupon, Schnellinger sets himself up for a centre into the goalmouth that is as studied as a place kick. The ball goes in and Jack Charlton is in position to head it away, with

Held in attendance. The ball goes out to the right, and Haller, surging up, takes a long shot that goes wide of the goal.

Banks taps the goal-kick to Wilson, gathers the return, and makes a mighty punt out of it. The ball is cleared out of the rear German defence and goes to Emmerich, who feeds Overath. Emmerich then moves forward, but Overath knows he will go off-side, so he swings the ball across to the far side of the English penalty area where Seeler slips as he tries to turn on the ball. Wilson takes it and feeds Moore, who gives a pretty pass forward to Ball.

Ball's white legs flash as he goes over the turf. He is carrying the ball, as if tiredness did not exist for him. He veers left, and then comes back right, unbalancing Weber. From twenty yards out, Ball has to struggle not just to shoot but to make his shot so accurate that a leaping Tilkowski must knock it over the bar.

Then Ball races out to the flag to take the corner kick – he is like a kid new to the game. Weber heads the corner away, and as it comes out Cohen is there to tackle Emmerich. But the Germans regain possession as Haller sends it forward and to the right to Beckenbauer. For once, the cool Beckenbauer misses the pass. Has he noticed that Schnellinger has come to a dead halt because of cramp? But Beckenbauer hurries to his right to rescue the ball – it is evident now, in midfield especially, that there is much free space: coverage has been overcome by tiredness. Beckenbauer passes to Held, who gives it to Emmerich. He prepares to take a booming, long shot, but Cohen closes on him, and at the right moment just turns his body so that the shot bounces off the back of his thigh.

Emmerich takes the throw-in to Overath, who puts in a small cross. But Wilson controls the ball and plays it away to Bobby Charlton. Beckenbauer drags himself to within notional coverage range, but Bobby is nearly scornful. He advances, moving inside, knowing that brother Jack is coming up outside him to the left. Then, at the nice moment, he slips the ball across to Jack – Beckenbauer is no more than an on-looker to this. Jack, just like a winger, takes the ball on his left foot and crosses it quickly right into the heart of the goal area where Hurst so challenges Tilkowski in the air that the German keeper can only tip the ball sideways so that it goes out of play for a throw.

Ball throws in, to Hunt, who holds it a second and then gives it back to Ball. He crosses. Peters, awkwardly, heads the ball. A German, Schulz, heads again, and Peters, regaining his balance, takes the ball to the ground and slides it back to Bobby Charlton, on the edge of the penalty area. Bobby has a view for a shot, and he delivers a terrific drive low and to Tilkowski's left. The keeper dives and the ball strikes him – in the face, it seems – and is turned on to the post. This is, at best, a lucky save, and the most dangerous thing Bobby has done all day.

Weber gathers the ball, and gives it out to Emmerich, who feeds Held. The Germans seem ready for a fast break, but Cohen intervenes and the Germans fall back on inter-passing. Overath gives to Haller, and then Held passes to Emmerich. But urgency is withering, and Stiles is able to step in, take the ball, and deliver it safely back to Banks.

Banks feeds Wilson out on the left, and he passes forward to Hunt, who moves inside and sends a long but threatening right-foot shot across the face of the goal. It goes harmlessly for a goal-kick, but Hunt seems energetic still and yet again there was room for danger. The German coverage is nowhere near as tight as England's.

Tilkowski's long goal-kick is easily cleared by Stiles. It goes by way of Hunt to Hurst. He passes back to Moore, who returns it, deep to the left to Hunt, who is able to run round Schulz and put in a shot that Höttges turns away for a corner.

And now, as Ball runs across the field to take another corner, a brilliant sun comes out, the best of the day. This casts long shadows and shines in Tilkowski's eyes: he puts on a cap. Weber clears Ball's corner. It comes out to Bobby Charlton, who passes to Wilson. But Schulz knocks his cross away, and Overath suddenly sees a long pass to Seeler on the right. He quickly crosses to

Emmerich running up on the left – the English defence has been caught moving up, and unbalanced to their left. But the opening is lost as Emmerich holds on too long instead of passing back crisply to Seeler. As it is, the ball goes from Emmerich to Held, but Stiles takes it away from him and Held fouls Stiles as he tries to recover.

'Eng-*land*! Eng-*land*!' The volleys of noise come out of the crowd. They are not just encouraging. They are demanding.

'We're going to do it,' says my friend. 'I know we are.' Then he gives me a sidelong look, and he says, 'Aren't we?'

'We always have before,' I assure him.

22

Geoff Hurst was your average boy football player, and he was about to become an ideal. He was born in December 1941, in Ashton-under-Lyne, a suburb to the east of Manchester. His Dad, Charlie Hurst, was a notably small centre-half who played for Oldham. When Geoff was six, the family moved to Chelmsford, and the Dad, slipping a bit as a player, became a part-time professional with Chelmsford as well as a tool-maker. Geoff would write later of his childhood, 'I was playing with a ball every chance I got, and used to come into the house at dusk absolutely exhausted.' In the late 1940s, that only described a few million lads, for kicking a ball about then was automatic.

He played in the back garden. His Dad coached him in the basic skills. He played with other kids in the street, and learned the tricky art of playing the ball off the kerb. Once, he and some other boys were called up in court and fined for persistently kicking the ball into a neighbour's garden. It happened. Most neighbours were patient and forgiving, so long as your parents paid up for the broken windows. But all of us knew the contrite, breathless way of saying, 'Excuse me, could I have my ball back?' The ball, that precious thing! A Christmas present, so awkwardly wrapped, and then religiously loaded with Dubbin and taken to the bicycle shop to be kept pumped up.

Geoff never stopped practising. I don't know about the rest of his education – his book doesn't mention it. He played for his school, then for Chelmsford Schools. He and his Dad even played together for Halstead in the Essex Border League, and he got a trial with West Ham. They became his team, and he was theirs: at the time of the World Cup, nine of the eleven England players were with the clubs that had found them as youths and developed them. Only Gordon Banks and Ray Wilson had ever been transferred, from a lower-division team to a more appropriate higher level of play.

Hurst worked his way up through the West Ham organisation. He was diligent, willing, hard-working, and coachable. He grew big and strong. He had a friendly grin. But he was not the best wing-half in a team that had Bobby Moore and then Martin Peters. So the West Ham manager coaxed him into the forward line, and then, when Johnny Byrne came to West Ham from Crystal Palace, they formed a partnership. But Geoff had never thought of himself as a star. He had happily painted the grandstand as a junior. He worked on being extra-fit to keep up with those he regarded as superior players. Nor did he make his debut for England, until the February 1966 game against West Germany. He was over-awed on the England squad. Alf Ramsey had had to tell him to speak out more, to call to the others that he wanted the ball. Deserved it. But Alf trusted quiet men. And the trust was about to be repaid.

England have a free kick on the edge of the goal area because of Held's foul on Stiles. Cohen taps the ball back to Banks, and he rolls it out to Bobby Moore on the left. Moore passes down the wing, studiously, to Hurst. It is a good ball, but Höttges beats Hurst with a clever turn that draws applause from the English crowd. Hurst has always known defenders who could take him.

Höttges passes to Overath, who gives it down the right wing to Haller. But, for once, Haller can't see what to do. He makes an impatient gesture – no-one is running off the ball for him – and slips it back to Overath. He passes square to Schnellinger, who moves it farther left to the advancing Beckenbauer. Beckenbauer tries a long shot, but Stiles turns and lets the kick bounce off his bottom. It goes to Schnellinger, who gives it out to Overath on the right. He crosses the ball, but Jack Charlton easily picks it off in the air.

That clearance goes to Peters, who slips the ball forward to Hunt. He then makes a rapid diagonal advance, carrying the ball – he seems as strong as ever – and gives it on to Hurst, who is expertly tackled by Schulz. He gives it to Schnellinger, who passes back to Tilkowski, who now looks dashing in his cap.

The keeper throws the ball out to Overath. He gives it to Haller and takes the return. Then from Overath it goes to Seeler, who also gives it back. The German attacks are cloaked with an air of deference now, a reluctance to be bold or decisive. Overath then swings the ball across-field to Beckenbauer, who advances promisingly only to lose control of the ball, letting it roll on to Peters.

Peters passes to Hurst, who gives the ball out to Bobby Moore on the right, but Moore is comprehensively tackled by Schulz, who sends the ball out of play.

Moore sends the throw-in to Wilson, and takes the return. He puts in a cross, but Weber easily gathers the ball and sends it clear to Haller. In turn, he passes out to Held on the left. The situation here seems ordinary enough, but Held starts to advance down the left, running into the setting sun, the grass burnished before him. He goes past Ball first, and then as Jack Charlton comes to cover him, so Held summons up strength and will and summarily by-passes Jack on the outside. He is all the way to the goal-line, where he puts in a pretty dangerous cross that passes all the way across the face of the English goal – begging, nearly hesitating – but finds no-one eager or determined enough just to be there to meet it with the requisite wallop or touch. As he has indicated from time to time, Held has it in him to roll up the English defence from the left. But here a goal was to be had. Banks watches the cross go by like a man who has narrowly missed an accident.

Bobby Charlton gathers the loose ball and gives it to Hunt.

It comes back to Bobby, who passes upfield to Hunt, who is, as it were, habitually dispossessed by Weber. The ball goes out of play, and Hunt takes the throw-in, to Wilson. He picks up on the return and puts in a cross, but the ball goes harmlessly into the side netting with Tilkowski guarding the near post.

The sun is still intense, that glorious, golden five o'clock look of an English summer, enough to make one lament that soccer isn't a summer game, played in the evenings on dry pitches.

Tilkowski's goal-kick goes wide to the right, to Haller, who has to twist awkwardly to head the ball. It goes to Bobby Charlton, who gives a nice sideways pass to Stiles – Stiles and Bobby both have their socks down now – who sends it forward to Hunt, who is cleanly tackled by the excellent Weber, who clears the ball away, but only to Bobby Charlton.

Bobby looks to the right again, and to Stiles, who lays the ball off for the advancing Cohen. At this point, Cohen and Ball are nearly side-by-side down the right wing. So Cohen gives the short pass to Ball, who takes it past Emmerich and then outside Schnellinger before tapping it sideways to his shadow, Cohen, whose cross passes ineptly behind the goal. If alone, Ball would surely have been more dangerous.

We are ten minutes into the first half of extra time.

Tilkowski rolls the ball out to Schulz, who passes it back to the keeper, so that he can punt away deep into the England half. Jack Charlton heads it away to Stiles, who gathers the ball well inside his own half. And now fatigue and uncertainty are gone for a few seconds. There will be three English efforts now – the ball kicked three times – and each one is perfection.

Stiles does not so much look up and judge as *know* that Ball is moving forward down the right. So Stiles gives him a pass, thirty yards through the air, and dropping down beyond Schnellinger's chase, that would be acutely placed for a Ball as fresh as the first minute of a new game.

That is not this Alan Ball. The pass lands five yards ahead of his run. It seems to gain another yard on him as it runs. But then, from somewhere, Ball grabs hold of greater need or zest. He accelerates. He closes on the ball. He must be so extended he is beyond thought. Anyone in this situation, surely, would gather the ball, look up, and take a half-second of rest — enough for a defence to regather. Ball only meets the ball ahead of him, and as he does so, crosses it. There is so often a moment in soccer when what you do is less vital than doing it immediately, or a beat sooner than anyone else reckoned.

The cross, bending backwards a little, finds Hurst two yards away from the corner of the six-yard box, with Schulz scrambling a couple of steps beyond him.

Hurst traps the ball beautifully with his right foot — you can almost hear a Dad's voice coaching him through the move. He then swivels, lets the ball bounce a couple of times, lightly, no more than a few inches, makes a slight adjustment in his body-weight, and still in the turn, delivers a stunning, drive shot with his right foot.

Tilkowski is on the goal-line. A greater goalkeeper would have come out, narrowing the angle, hoping to smother the shot. But Tilkowski comes only one step, and stops. His knees are bent; he is ready to go down for a low shot.

But Hurst is falling back as he shoots, and so the angle of the shot carries it over a Tilkowski who is trying to straighten, trying to lean back as the ball passes over him. He is very close to touching it, but the shot is too violent.

Hurst is falling over backwards, to compensate for the thrust of his shot.

The ball hits the underside of the cross-bar. Very forcefully.

It bounces down, on or around the goal-line.

Back-spin carries it back into the field of play where Weber, coming in behind Hunt, heads it away — for a corner?

There is confusion, that lasts till this day.

Hurst believes that the ball 'hit up in the roof of the net, touching where the cross-bar and net were joined'. But that ball would have bounced down, more softly, into the net. This one hit nothing but bar, even if the exact underside of what is a rounded bar.

According to the rules of the game, for this shot to be a goal, the entirety of the ball must be over the goal-line. If a part of the ball hit the line, then the ball remained in play.

Some say that Hunt, who was in a good position to see, held back, as if to say – the ball was in, it was a goal. But the film does not make this clear. Hunt hesitates, as if in uncertainty, and is then beaten by the more decisive Weber, as he was all afternoon.

The referee is not sure what has happened. There are a few seconds of indecision in the goalmouth, with English players claiming a goal, and Germans waving it off. There should be no question, however, about the comprehensive impact of the move. Even if the law rescued them, the Germans are shattered.

Then Herr Dienst runs to the sideline, to talk to the linesman, Tofik Bahkramov, a Russian. These two men do not have a language in common. They talk, with players all around them. The referee emerges, and moves towards the centre of the field. For a kick-off. Goal. 3–2.

The film coverage was not then as extensive as it would be now. Even so, one would need a camera in the goal on the line, or one of those electronic lines that spy movies love, to determine exactly what happened.

It is my estimate that it was not quite or entirely a goal. A part of the ball was on the line.

But let me add two things. This was, so far, the best 'goal' of the match, and there is an irrepressible merit or logic in such great soccer that should not be denied. I mean by that that referee and linesman, with only their eyes to go by, saw a piece of wonder and violent execution that they could not reason away.

Then there is the fact that the referee decided it was a goal. Errors given such sweet power are very hard to bear – like the goal against England that Maradona punched in for Argentina in the Mexico World Cup of 1986. 'The hand of

God', Maradona called it. And it was given as a goal. And Argentina beat us, 2–1.

There is no playing of any game unless the players and everyone else know that the referee, the umpire, whatever, can be wrong, and will be sometimes, but must be honoured. It is at such moments that the weight of a lifetime, the drama of the crowd and the occasion, and every atom of human desire must know how to stand back and say, well, this is only a game. And in the end, a game is a foolish enterprise without significance.

'I was never out,' the batsman says as he walks past the umpire who has given him the finger.

'Ah-ha,' says the umpire, 'look in the papers tomorrow.'

There is geometry and physics in a ball bouncing off a given surface. But there is chance in how men see it, and what they decide they saw.

3–2. Stiles to Ball to Hurst – a glorious movement.

And twenty minutes still to play.

23

The Germans kick off again. They are only a goal down. They have been there already, as well as a goal up, so they know how quickly equality can be restored. But they have been out-played for most of an hour now, and they are very weary. No wonder then, if they have a feeling like that of the professional German Army once the landings of D-Day had been established. Which is not to say that the Germans will not fight, or remain unusually dangerous, believing in luck and English errors, but still they will be professional about it and begin to estimate how much longer and what to do afterwards. A side in that situation must begin to tidy up in its own mind: it cannot allow the last moments of defeat to strip it down further, to discover nakedness, abject terror or self-pity. You must be professional about losing. You look for honour and dignity and closing that book. It is the necessary way of preparing for the next struggle. And West Germany handle this very well – their World Cup record after 1966 is going to be so much better than England's.

Is winning harder or more testing than losing? Well into the 1960s – indeed, especially in the period just after the World Cup, when sterling had to be devalued – one heard the rueful English wondering as to whether it wouldn't have been better, or shrewder, to lose the Second World War. After all, hadn't the 'free world' bent over backwards after 1945 to re-build and re-energise Japan and West Germany so that they were 'robust' democracies again? While England, sad England, dwindled and shrank and generally behaved like a wounded veteran of war, never its old self again.

The Wembley crowd now is singing, 'Britain never, never, never shall be slaves'. Of course, there's an irony there that most Brits don't notice. British experience of 'slavery', or of being ruled by others, stopped with the Norman Conquest, an invasion that helped enrich the land and the culture in so many ways. Thereafter, on and off, the English could tell themselves that the French or the Spanish or the Germans might invade — and so they sent armies to make war in Europe. English people might hear the noise of artillery bombardments drifting over the Channel with the mist in the years 1914–18, but English fields were not made burial grounds. The Armada was a famous English victory. Napoleon was trounced by Nelson and Wellington: whereas few English kids are ever taught what Napoleon did to alter government and thinking in Europe. Similarly, the Second World War for Britain is 'The Few', in Spitfires and Hurricanes, picking off German bombers in 1940; it is El Alamein, D-Day, the Ardennes and the taking of Germany. It is not really the struggle between Fascism and Communism, or the attack on the Jews.

So the valiantly upheld avoidance of slavery rings out in 'Rule Britannia!' despite the effective enslavement of whole peoples in Africa, India and Asia by that thing called the British Empire. To say nothing of the British role — individual and collective — in the slave-trade between Africa and the Americas. Instead, the British treasure a man called William Wilberforce and their own early abolition of slavery. Equally, in the 1950s and early 1960s, British pride was congratulating itself on feeling the wind of change and 'granting' freedom to the new nations of Africa — though the awkwardness in Rhodesia was an exception to that magnanimous grace, and the door-step to South Africa.

Then there were other kinds of servitude, things about Britain that I found repellent or ridiculous, and always depressing. When I was ten, I got a scholarship to Dulwich College. There were about

1,200 boys at Dulwich then, and I'd guess that three-quarters of that number were there on scholarships, most of them paid for by the London County Council. Naturally, it had once been a school (what the British call a public school) where nearly all the students paid for their places. But the school had grown old-fashioned. During the Labour Government of 1945–51, it had had to make a deal whereby it was given money for new buildings and equipment – notably the Science Block – in return for granting places to poor kids who could not otherwise afford to be at the school.

I felt lucky, and I still do, for it was then a fine school (despite the absence of girls) and a terrific education. But on my first day there, the new boys – about 200 of us – were assembled before the Deputy Master. He told us that we were supposed to be 'the cream of South London – but unfortunately the cream has gone a little sour these days'. No-one laughed out loud, or stoned the man. We meekly took the rebuke, and settled into the status of ordinary rankers bizarrely promoted beyond our station. To illustrate that a little further, there was an occasion in my last year at Dulwich when I had been made a prefect, and I was part of the assembly in the prefects' room that witnessed the captain of the school beating another boy – a contemporary of mine, someone I had been friendly with – on the bottom with a cane, for insolence to another prefect. This was permitted. It was a required spectacle for the other prefects. And so a gang of eighteen-year-olds saw a youth of the same age driven to public tears because he had said something cheeky (it may even have been witty) to a contemporary, which amounted to offence because that contemporary was a prefect.

Dulwich taught hierarchy then. One knew, one felt, which boys could pay for their places. There was also the system of academic and athletic rating: some people were more a credit to the school than others. I did well on both those scores, but I hated the underlying notion that there was a God-given or God-ordained place for everyone – and in a grim, agnostic way,

God was much around as a kind of adjunct to the captain of the school.

I loathed a system of such early placement, and I despised those who obeyed it. No matter how steadily the English made comedy of their class system – and this is often classic comedy – they could not rid themselves of it, or the depression that went with being born downcast. There were so many jobs or ways of life for which some immense qualification – land, birth, money, accent, having been to University, class – was essential. There were unspoken, invisible barriers that it was gauche folly to try crossing. My life was not hard in many ways. I was lucky in most things. But I can see now that I was particularly angry about the enclosures of class because I could not utter the anger I felt about the way my father lived. Don't ask, he was saying silently. Keep your place.

What has this got to do with the World Cup of 1966, you may be asking? I'm not sure I can give you a lucid or simple answer, but I know it's the question that made me want to write this book. You see, I think England's victory in 1966 was a great emotional release, far more than a professional accomplishment. It wasn't really a way of winning systematically, or by habit, it was the chance – if only for a moment – to escape self-pity and the gloom of irony at being good losers; it was a way of shouting out and stomping on someone. It was a moment in the early, heady 1960s, when real freedoms seemed at hand, of saying, this could be a new Britain, classless, unburdened by modesty and the need to be 'gentlemen', and ready to be men who win! It seemed to me a proof of something I was struggling to define, let alone believe in – that if you wanted something, to be a writer, to be happy, to feel free, it was up to you to go out there and lay hands on it. And at least explain how your father's life had been an elaborate, cruel farce – not just for the wife he had left, but for the woman (the 'love' of his life?) who had to do without him two weekends in three, and every Christmas, Easter, and bank holiday. Much later, I learned that that woman was – or said she was – an orphan. So she had every Christmas for thirty years on her own. My father had put us all in a kind of prison and dared us to complain.

I never did – until near the end of his life. I witnessed the prefect's beating without saying, 'This is monstrous'. I was a child who stammered close to the point of silence, and in my twenties I was beginning to suffer from what I would learn later was depression. I had to learn to win. And win again. Secure in the knowledge that everyone loses in the end.

So Germany kick off again. Haller gives it to Overath, who gives it to Schnellinger. The full-back sends in a deep cross that Jack Charlton (as ever) heads away. Peters takes the ball in the air and flicks it away towards the touchline. Beckenbauer runs after it and sends back another cross that is once more headed away by Jack. But this clearance bounds off Bobby Moore and goes straight back to Banks, all in a twinkle, when another kind of bounce could have put it in the goal.

Banks throws it out to Hunt. He passes to Bobby Charlton, who finds Hurst, all inside the English half. He gives it to Peters, who beats Beckenbauer only to see Overath pick up the ball. He sends it to Emmerich, who gives it back to him. He then sends the ball across-field to the right, to Beckenbauer, who slips the harassing Ball and passes out to Schnellinger. Again, the full-back prepares to cross the ball, but the advancing Wilson takes it flush on the forehead, staggering, and goes down. Wilson will say later that he was stunned for several minutes – in a daze. Heading the ball is not as easy as writing that phrase. There was a time when footballs were just leather, when they absorbed moisture and mud, and grew heavier as the game went on. Latex paint has reduced that risk – in the old days it was not uncommon to see a defender knocked out by heading a hard shot. And now, assessing weight and velocity, doctors are even realising that persistent heading may cause damage in the way that some boxers suffer injuries to the brain. It is argued that Danny Blanchflower – dead of Alzheimer's disease at the age of sixty-seven – may have been such a victim. Or maybe it was just that he was once the best talker who ever played the game.

Beckenbauer gathers the rebound from Wilson's brow and sends the ball leftward to Overath. He gives it to Haller, who frees Held on the left wing. Once more, Held thinks about flanking the defence, but Peters tackles him very tidily, and as Held tries to regain the ball so he fouls Peters.

Cohen sends the free kick back to Banks. He gives it to Wilson – who is playing on – and he passes it on to Ball. Ball gives it to Bobby Charlton, who holds and lingers with the ball, letting time pass. No German closes in to challenge him. But Moore moves up outside Bobby, takes the pass, considers briefly, and rolls it back to Bobby, who then kicks it into the German goal area.

Schulz clears the ball to Haller, who slips it left so that Cohen swings at the passing ball but misses it. This frees Emmerich for a run, but Cohen recovers rapidly, sneaks up on the ball and makes to kick it away for a corner. But Banks is so alert as to save this 'shot'.

He gives it out to Bobby Charlton, who feeds Stiles. He passes to Ball, who beats Overath and makes a pass out to the right wing that Schnellinger deliberately blocks with his hand.

Ball takes the free kick and gives it to Bobby Charlton, who kicks the ball forward speculatively, only to see it run out of play. In fact, to save time, Tilkowski runs over to field it – the ball crosses the goal-line, but he is allowed to gather it up and pass away to save time. On this occasion, the Russian linesman is not consulted.

Tilkowski's punt finds Haller, who gives it out to Held, now on the right wing. Jack Charlton is tracking Held, but the German is able to swing the ball all the way across-field to Emmerich, who sends in a long, powerful left-foot shot that goes over the far post, still rising.

Banks takes the goal-kick and gives it to Moore. He feeds Hurst, and the ball is sleepily triangulating Hunt, Peters and Moore when the referee blows for half-time in extra time. Trainer Les Cocker comes on to the field and bathes Ray Wilson's face in cold water. Alf is there, chatting to Bobby Moore. Wilson's face looks raw and battered, but Moore is as cool and impassive as when the game began. Does Alf say, 'Never, never be slaves,' or 'Don't muck it up'?

24

In the brief interlude between the two halves of extra time, Alf is seen on the field, with a word here and there for players. Some portions of the crowd pick up the chant, 'Ram-sey, Ram-sey,' for there is a general acceptance now that England are where they are because of discipline, effort and coaching. All that remains is that basic activity of these men's lives – kick the ball around for fifteen minutes or so – without losing control. And so the ordinary motions of the game – the foot that kills the ball and makes it obedient, the side-foot pass that goes within a yard of its intended destination – the automatic moving into space, the calculation of a ball's flight and bounce – all these things become golden and engraved, the ways of habit given grace and eternity. And as you watch, or as I try to narrate the course of the game, you feel the nearly religious significance that occurred sometime in the nineteenth century when football and rugby split, and some elected to handle the ball, while others drove their minds and their souls into their legs and feet and regarded 'hands' as a sin. It is worth noting that soccer begins with a deliberate and voluntary acceptance of a kind of handicap that may eventually foster a sublime skill.

It may seem folly to honour every kick, or nearly every kick, in a whole game, with extra time, especially when we all know the result. But this game is history, like the Bayeux Tapestry, and because, in the last analysis, the suspense is not there, so it is easier to absorb the ordinary, dance-like beauty of what passes.

As England kick off, Bobby Charlton's touch to Hurst is so dainty, some German defenders believe that Hurst has simply charged forward with the ball. They wait for a whistle. So he goes a dozen yards before Overath intervenes and removes the ball from him. Then Overath slides it forward to Beckenbauer, who passes leftward to Emmerich, who moves it on to Held. He would advance, but Jack Charlton, his gloomy shadow now, closes in and puts the ball out of play. Held seems diffident about engaging Jack physically.

Held throws in to Emmerich and is waiting for the return when Cohen intrudes and snaps the ball away. His rapid clearance goes straight to Schnellinger, who gives the ball to Overath. He passes on to Emmerich, but Jack puts in the tackle and as the ball runs free, Cohen once more tidies it up.

He chips the ball down the English right, where Hurst controls it on his chest and neatly supplies Ball, who sets off across field and then strokes a long pass all the way out to the left, to Hunt. He sets off doggedly down the left, but Schulz waits for him and then separates him from the ball. But it runs free again, and the insatiable Ball is there to pick it up. He turns in, towards the middle of the field, and then exuberantly back-heels the ball towards Wilson, overlapping on the left. It is so cheeky a flick that it shows Ball's certainty of victory.

Wilson is harassed by Schulz near the corner, but still he manages to step back and deliver a right-foot cross that Weber heads away.

This goes to Beckenbauer, who now seems to run the midfield. He is seldom hurried – indeed, he is the German who has the rather languid pace of the English holding on to a lead – but he looks increasingly effective as a designer of plays. He is storing up his future. He gives it left, to Held, who tries a fine upfield pass, meant for Emmerich, that is boldly cut off by Jack Charlton.

He sends it wide to the right, to Hunt, who is easily robbed by Höttges. He sends the ball square to Schulz, who prods it forward, again, to Beckenbauer, who now advances. As he comes, he swerves round Bobby Charlton without much trouble, and tries a long shot – low, rolling, insignificant – that is mere practice for Banks. It is an oddity, but Beckenbauer's goals, early in the Cup, seem to have swayed him from his true purpose, to conceive goals for others. Banks rolls it out to Moore. He gives it to Hunt and takes the return. Moore's plan now, the sun bright on his blond hair, is to seem immaculate and serene. Just to be evidence of mastery. He has a calling for it: it is as if his great ambition on the field is to be exemplary and reassuring. He passes to Bobby Charlton, who sends it square to Peters, who delivers it outside to Hurst. He and Peters exchange passes, as in an exercise, before a Hurst lob is mis-timed and Overath seizes the ball, running it out of play. Cohen throws in to Stiles, who advances, like a devout dribbler, before he is tackled nimbly by Overath. But the ball runs free, to Hurst, who puts in a respectable snap shot, just to remind Tilkowski that this is a real match.

The goalkeeper throws it wide to the right, to Seeler, who slips Ball and boots it upfield. But Held, the eager recipient, has been played off-side and his excitement turns to sourness.

Moore sends the free kick to Cohen. He gives it to Hunt, who passes to Hurst. But Schnellinger takes it away and passes to Beckenbauer, who gives a short, deferring sideways pass to Held. He then passes to Emmerich, but again Jack Charlton clears. The ball goes to Moore, who passes to Ball, who slips it inside to Bobby Charlton. Whereupon, Bobby, with deft élan, sends a first-time left-foot ball deep into . . . nowhere, but the German defence. Bobby is so magical sometimes, yet he's always capable of this sort of aimless, unconsidered action. Yet he's always forgiven, for the world loves him.

Schulz gathers the stray ball. He moves it forward to Emmerich, who gives to Beckenbauer, who finds Overath. He then tries a bold pass, wide to the right, to Haller. But the pass is inaccurate:

instead of leading Haller on, it passes behind him and goes out of play.

Moore takes the throw-in, erect and classical, to Ball. He gives it back to Moore, who passes to Wilson. The full-back considers a move forward, but feels less than secure and so turns back and passes to Banks. Even now, holding on for the ultimate victory, the English fans whistle at this timidity. The back pass to the keeper cannot be outlawed, but we should always remember that once it was disdained.

Banks punts the ball away down the middle of the field, and Weber rises to head it clear. That ball goes to Overath, but it rolls away to Bobby Charlton, who releases Hunt on the left. Hunt runs on and runs into the implacable Schulz. He falls over and seems to expect a whistle, but in truth, at this stage, you have to be more skilful than Hunt is to get such a call. Schulz simply beat him – and the referee has been watching this game long enough to take that for granted.

But so has Ball. For he is there waiting to pounce on Schulz's tackle and scoop up the free ball. He then sends a nice, threatening square ball across the outer line of the penalty area. Peters has a flicker of a chance with it, but Beckenbauer comes back, takes the ball, and guides it to Tilkowski.

Tilkowski pauses and then throws the ball out to the advancing Beckenbauer. He slips the ball left, to Held, who cuts inside, where Peters tackles him. The ball bounds clear to Beckenbauer, who tries another shot. This is blocked by an English defender.

It runs away as far as Bobby Charlton, who finds Stiles on the right. He advances and moves it on to Ball, who canters outside Schnellinger, turns a pretty reverse circle, and slips the ball out to Stiles coming up outside him during the circling manoeuvre. Stiles is free, but his cross fades away behind the goal.

Tilkowski's goal-kick goes to Schulz, who passes forward to Emmerich. He touches it back to Haller, who then finds Beckenbauer. He sends it right to Overath, who plays it back to the left. Emmerich feints to take this pass, but lets it run on to Held, who then charges at goal, beating two men, Cohen and Stiles, before Peters tackles him. Peters kicks it away to the right, and the ball goes out of play.

We are half-way through the last half of extra time.

'So,' I turn to my friend – he has another of his home-made cigarettes hanging from his lower lip. 'What are you going to do if we win?'

His eyes brighten in a modest way. 'What am I going to do?'

'Right.'

'Well, I'll tell you, I'll put a few pints away tonight, wouldn't be surprised.'

'Take the wife out?'

'Wouldn't reckon.'

'Not her thing?'

'She doesn't like the drinking.'

'So, out with the lads, then?'

He gives me a shy grin.

'Oh, yeah, there'll be a crowd. Don't you worry.'

But there is a wistful, lonesome ring to his voice, a kind of echo not much used to company.

'But,' I add gravely, 'you won't be running wild on the streets, Molotov-cocktailing parked cars and seizing on defenceless women?'

'Nah, shouldn't imagine. What's the point?'

'Burn down a public building?'

'Nah, not my style, squire.'

'No outrages against civic dignitaries?'

'You're having me on.'

'But shouldn't we go wild?'

He reflects. 'Might be nice,' he says in a far-away voice. 'But I'll tell you one thing.'

'Yeah?'

'My grandson.'

'Yeah?'

'He's only two, nipper.'

'Right.'

'I'll tell him I was here.'

'Good!'

'Got a programme for him.'

'He'll love it.'

'However.'

'Yeah?'

'I won't tell him about you.'

'You won't?'

'And knowing about 1975 and such.'

'Ah, you know . . .'

'Nah, mate,' he chuckles. 'I won't tell him anything about the nutter I was stood next to.'

'Take care of that boy,' I say. 'Hard times coming.'

'Don't tell me about hard times, mate,' he says. 'And you take care of yours.'

25

Hurst takes the throw-in, out on the English right. He directs it to Bobby Charlton, who sends a short pass to Ball. Haller moves in, and Ball makes a gesture at a jinking pass that draws a foul from Haller. The German is apologetic, not least because of the extra time consumed. Bobby Charlton taps the free kick to Ball and then runs on to gather the extra touch from a Ball who is at last ready to take a rest. Bobby puts in a deep cross along the eighteen-yard line. Peters gets his head to it, but not in a way he can control. Weber picks up the loose ball – has Weber made a mistake yet? – and slips it forward to Beckenbauer. He guides it left, to Emmerich, who touches it on to Held. Held makes to cut inside, but then he elects to shoot, and the ball goes high over the goal. The crowd murmurs and flutters in self-congratulation that one more German effort has been nullified.

Banks's goal-kick reaches deep into the German half. Schulz's header bounds back and is gathered in by Bobby Charlton, who sends a short, sidelong pass to Stiles so that he can emphatically boot it out of play to the left – or did he see a friend in the crowd and send a salute?

Weber takes the throw-in and gives it to Beckenbauer, who is now the pivot in nearly every German attack. He passes left to Held – if not the most dangerous German, clearly the most energised still – and Held drives the ball forward. It hits Jack Charlton, and as the rebound comes to him, Held deftly controls it with his hand. He could have been through, but about 90,000 people see the offence.

The free kick goes back to Banks, who lofts the ball away. Weber heads it clear, to Overath, to Beckenbauer, who slides it right to Seeler. But Wilson blocks his shot, and the ball comes to Moore, who frees Hunt down the left. Hunt carries the ball deep into German territory and then sends it square to the right to Hurst. Hurst plays the ball forward, past one German defender, but so strongly that it carries all the way to Tilkowski. It is clear now that the Germans are leaving fewer people back in defence, so that every assault upon them seems to have space to work in – as well as weary legs to beat.

Tilkowski throws the ball to Beckenbauer, who lays it off for an advancing Schulz. He plays the ball forward, as if for Held, but Jack Charlton makes a lunging cut-off. This sends the ball straight to Emmerich, who plays it on for Held before Jack can recover. The English defenders allege off-side, but the referee refuses them. Held advances and puts in a dangerous cross that is contested by Seeler and Wilson. Their heads clash: both men seem hurt. And the ball goes for a corner. Without Wilson's pressure, Seeler had a clear chance at goal.

The corner is played short to Beckenbauer and his deep cross is cleverly cleared by Cohen's anticipation. He gives it to Ball, who sends it to Hunt. From him it goes to Bobby Charlton, and so to Moore, who sets Hunt free, advancing from the left. From about 22 yards away Hunt delivers a powerful, swerving shot that just beats the far post.

Tilkowski sends the goal-kick short to Höttges, who passes it on to Emmerich. He finds Schnellinger, but the ball bounces clear to Bobby Charlton, who passes to Ball. Then Ball's advance is thwarted as Beckenbauer darts in and sends a safe ball back to Tilkowski.

The keeper throws it out to Overath, who gives it, going left, to Beckenbauer (so rapidly back on the attack). Beckenbauer moves it right, to Haller, who feints to shoot, then rolls it back to Beckenbauer, who now goes the other way, to Held. Held takes the ball past Stiles and puts in a fast cross that hits Emmerich's foot and goes over the goal-line. Held remains a menace, but nothing he starts is being finished by others.

Yet again, Banks settles for an old-fashioned kick-away. Hurst rises to nod it on, so that the ball rolls towards the German left corner flag, where Schulz must scurry to recover it. He passes up the left to Emmerich, who passes to Schnellinger and is then flattened in a collision with Stiles. Schnellinger sends the ball to the right, to Seeler, who plays it back to Weber. His cross is booted away by a Stiles who somehow came out of the collision with Emmerich unruffled, and innocent.

People are saying there are four minutes left – some say it is only a blink, others feel it as an eternity.

Weber takes the throw-in and sends it to Haller, who has to put a sly hand on the ball's big bounce. But not sly enough. 'Hands!' that corner of the ground cries – like kids at a pantomime.

Moore takes the free kick and sends the ball to Hunt. He plays it off, square, to the right, to Hurst, who plays it back leftwards to Peters. He carries it on to Bobby Charlton, who sends it all the way to Ball on the left wing. Then we see a novelty: Ball is actually tackled by a German, by Beckenbauer in this case, who touches the ball on to Overath. He neatly evades Bobby Charlton's challenge and passes to Schnellinger. He feeds Seeler, who gives it back, going left, to Schnellinger. Then Schnellinger reverses direction and sends a long ball all the way across to the right. Caught unawares, Overath has to race to keep the ball in play. But he gets it and passes inside to Beckenbauer, who attempts a long shot.

This is resolutely headed away by Bobby Moore. But that ball only falls to Schnellinger, who gives it to Overath, then takes the return and puts in a deep cross. Jack Charlton clears this, but only to Held. But Held now is tackled by Roger Hunt, who sends the ball out of play.

Held gives the throw-in to Haller, who, far out on the left, decides to put in a snap centre. This drops in Banks's arms, as if in a boys' kick-about someone decided that Gordon was being left out of the fun.

Banks throws clear to Hurst, who plays it off to Ball. He makes a nice forward, diagonal pass to the left, for Peters, but Schulz has seen it coming and he easily gathers the ball. Then he sends it left to Overath, who gives it to Beckenbauer, and on to Emmerich. He sends it away right to the advancing Schulz. His cross, going to the far post, England's right, is artfully headed down by Haller – to fall in Seeler's path. All of a sudden, with moments left, Germany could have an equaliser. But the ball runs half a step too fast for Seeler and goes away to the right. Schulz takes it and centres again, and Cohen carefully heads away for a corner.

More or less, granted the uncertainty of timing, there is a minute left to play. Haller takes the corner. Banks comes out for it, soars and punches it away. Will that be enough?

The ball goes out to Hurst, but Höttges is able to clear it. He sends it right, to Weber, who crosses once more. Moore controls it. He sends it to Hunt, who plays it back to Moore.

Moore seems ready to wait until someone compels him to do something. He might like to have the ball at the last whistle, then pick it up and say, 'Okay, lads, game's over. Let's get home for our tea.'

As if prompted, the referee looks at his watch and puts his whistle in his mouth.

The crowd sighs with rising wonder and expectation. The television coverage cuts in for a close-up of Herr Dienst.

But he feels this pressure and gives an impatient wave as if to say, 'Get on. Not yet. Not quite yet.' But he keeps his whistle in his mouth – no time to lose it.

So Moore, who has had a few seconds for a survey, sends a long, precise ball down the old inside-left track. To Hurst.

He is there, nearly alone. The ball bounces and then falls off his chest. It bounces again. He gathers it and turns, about ten yards inside the German half.

Ball is clear way out to his right.

Höttges is the only other German defender back. He feels Ball's presence and elects not to close on Hurst.

Meanwhile, Overath tries to fall back to get Hurst.

Geoff Hurst has never been an unequivocally great player. Never will be what we could call great – meaning the greatness of Di Stefano, Cruyff, Pelé, Law, Best, Puskas, Matthews and maybe a few others. But Geoff Hurst is a very good player, very well coached by everyone from his Dad to Ron Greenwood, and very good players by the luck of the numbers are going to have moments of ineffable splendour. Some are luckier than others in when those moments come.

Hurst carries the ball on, over a field that now looks like a meadow at the end of the day when a shoot has been held.

Overath is closing on him. But he is always too far.

Tilkowski is on the goal-line. But as some keepers try to make themselves large, Tilkowski seems ready to shrink.

Hurst is headlong, hurtling, and he has put the ball on his left. He is going to shoot. You feel it.

This is the kind of shot which, in weariness, nine out of ten very good players, ninety-nine times out of a hundred, would put in the stands to the cheery derision of the crowd.

But Geoff Hurst now is touched, cherry red in the golden light. He is for an instant Roy of the fucking Rovers. He draws back and shoots an insanely accurate, unstoppable, rising shot that goes past Tilkowski like an aircraft taking off and explodes against the roof of the net. The roof of the net in a shot from fifteen yards.

This is Belmonte taking a kill with one thrust. The muleta drawing the bull's head down, the sword a streak of brightness in the sun, then lost in the bull's darkness.

This is Fred Astaire beating back the noise his own feet make on the floor.

This is one of those moments you know all your life, by the light, the air, the feel, the force – like making love or seeing a baby squirm free of the mother's body, like seeing Montana's arm go up.

This is the goal that allows us all to forget the third goal that bounced on the line.

This is 4–2.

I roar in the living-room in Isleworth in front of the black-and-white TV. Mathew cannot quite yet know the grace that has touched Geoff Hurst. So he cries in alarm. But I was crying first. His mother comes into the room and tells me not to scare him so.

And I never have let him forget that moment and his less than fully-witting presence.

We have won.

AFTER TIME

Enough was enough, Herr Dienst decided. The Germans did not even get to kick off again. All over the land, people were going to the bathroom, walking out into the garden to breathe the air, dashing off to neglected shops before they closed. The collective kettle was being put on. Old balls were fetched out and kicked around in the noble knock-on of victory. At Wembley itself, the sun was out again, and surely no-one in England can remember anything other than the glow of a summer evening that had hours to go yet.

The English players gathered at the touchline closest to their team bench and the stairs to the Royal Box. Several of the reserves came out on to the field – Eastham, Gerry Byrne, Armfield, Callaghan, Bonetti, Connolly, Flowers – to be part of the joy. But they were dressed in coats and ties then – their readiness had never been an issue – and so they looked a little like players' brothers, accountants, bank clerks or pop singers, instead of people who had come so close to being soaked in sweat and the great shine of having come through.

Ramsey stayed back by the bench. He did not seem much affected, or surprised. He did not go wild, like King Kong with the wisp of Fay Wray in his grasp. He did not go berserk or lose it, whatever it was he had always had. Containment, thy name was Alf in the moments of victory. Of course, there were justifications: that they, the players, had done this, and that they

deserved their moment of community, of awe, tears and obscenity
– and Alf was not partial to coarse language; and that he, the Alf,
was not naturally ebullient or extravagant. So he waited until
protocol's officials indicated to the team that there was more
expected of them. They were to climb the steps that led up to
the Royal Box. And then Alf stood there – not exactly in their
way, but a little to one side, available – as the team passed by.
He and Moore put an arm around each other in passing. And
for the other players he had a word, a squeeze, a nod, a touch.
No more.

Bobby Moore led the team up the steps and then along the
walk-way in front of the Royal Box. As he makes the turn, going
from steps to walk-way, this chronic thinker-ahead sees a crisis
– as if Beckenbauer even now was fashioning deadly space for
himself. It is that he, even he, the unflappable one, the Skipper
who rarely needs to go at full pace, is by now a sweaty demon,
and there is Her Majesty, a few steps away, with gloves as white
as fresh chalk.

This does not defeat the Mooro. Without breaking stride, he
swipes his hands on shorts and shirt (he has likely had a friendly
quip rehearsed for weeks). But his garments are like clothes just
out of the wash. His hands come back moister than ever. What
then? The droll, innately dry Bobby just leans over and pats his
hands on the purple velvet that covers the front edge of the
Royal Box. And he does all this, cool and vanilla, as he's going
past the Kents, and Philip and Sir Stanley Rous. So there he is,
opposite the Queen, fit to shake her royal household gloves.

(Even then, a few of us wondered if he wasn't just making
ready to get a firm grip, so that he could throw the lady from
the box and declare the Republic then and there. After all, there
are moments for such things – and who knows how long we are
waiting now.)

Viscount Harewood is in the receiving line, and Harold Wilson
pops in his smiling face along with various officials of the football
world. And so the team troops by, waiting patiently for Moore to

hold aloft the Jules Rimet trophy, a solid piece of gold with a nice neck where it can be grasped. The line goes by after the skipper: Hurst, rather subdued; Bobby Charlton, in tears; Hunt, bemused; Peters, so young; Jack Charlton, tickled to be chatted to by all the nobs; Wilson, looking battered; Ball, using the balustrade for crutches nearly; Cohen, chipper; Stiles, letting the world see the gap in his teeth; and Gordon Banks, shy and downcast.

So the lads went down the other staircase, their backs beaten by fans leaning over to touch them. And then they gathered around Alf – he had not been up to see the Queen – and as the Marines struck up the National Anthem, so Alf could be seen, instructing or suggesting the proper way to handle a victory lap – not too fast at the outset, steady in the stretch, and then set for a big finish. There were photographers all over the place by then. Moore went up on his mates' shoulders. There were calls for Alf to join the group. He was reluctant, of course. But there are pictures that survive of Moore holding the Cup and Ramsey leaning towards it – did he mean to kiss the gold, or was he intent on blowing away fingerprints?

Then the players made their lap of honour, running around the perimeter of the ground, passing the trophy from hand to hand (though Moore stayed close, taking responsibility). Players searched out friends and wives in the crowd and waved to them. Nobby Stiles did his drunken sailor act. The players went up to the fence to show the Cup to standing throngs of English supporters. The flags in the crowd waved in response. And Alf Ramsey walked off the field and went back to the dressing-room.

The Marine band played, 'When the Saints Go Marching In' and plenty of the crowd sang along. Others tried, 'E-eye-addio-o, We Won the Cup'. And then after one last communion with the crowd by the tunnel, the men in red left their greatest green and went back into the gloom and the rest of their lives.

'Well, that's that,' said however many million people, settling into the rest of champions. And with it there must come a thought – we have won, we can relax, but if we ease off will we ever know how to win again?

I'm writing this on Monday, January 8th 1996 in San Francisco. Two days ago, on the Saturday afternoon at Candlestick Park, the San Francisco 49ers were beaten by the Green Bay Packers, 27–17 – in what amounts to the quarter-final leading to the Super Bowl.

I had an inkling this might happen. Though I had told my six-year-old son, Nicholas, that the 49ers were maybe the best team around, I warned him that Green Bay could beat us. The 49ers this season had a poor running game; their passing game relied too much on Jerry Rice; Steve Young had taken too much punishment all year. And, even so, when you looked at history closely you had to see that Young had never matched Joe Montana in the winning of desperate, close games where the 49ers had to come back from being behind.

I moved to San Francisco with my second wife, Lucy, in September 1981. That was the start of the season in which the 49ers, under the leadership of Bill Walsh, won their first Super Bowl. In the years since then, they have won five Super Bowls, and nearly every other year they have been in contention. They have had a chance and they have been worth watching. In that time they have had two great quarter-backs, Montana and Young, and a host of brilliant players and stalwart characters. Walsh retired, and was replaced with one of his assistants, George Seifert. The approach was maintained, the core of players was subtly renewed. Year in, year out, the team won and played spectacular, attacking football. Even this year, the 49ers scored more points in the regular season than any other team.

That sort of tradition of winning, over decades, is something that Manchester United and Liverpool have demonstrated in soccer. It is an extraordinary thing, dependent on ownership, management, coaching, training facilities, the players, the crowd, and the collective assumption that excellence can be maintained, along with the need to keep winning. On the other hand, in all sports in all countries, there are teams that have a brief moment of glory – Ipswich and Chelsea, say – a couple of great seasons – before sinking back into the pack of necessary losers. In all games, at the end of the season all but one team has lost. There is a constant need for losers if the thing is to work.

San Francisco now needs to rebuild, to regather itself, to renew its dedication – and a great organisation uses a losing season to spur that impasse. Thus, at Wembley, in all the jubilation of the winning day, let us not forget the start of a new campaign among the West German players.

Anyway, on Saturday afternoon, after we had watched the Green Bay loss on television, I stepped out into our garden for a moment and relaxed. If we had won, the next week's game, at Dallas, would have been a fearsome ordeal – we have no rivalry like the one with the Cowboys, and there is no game for which fans must be more dangerously screwed-up. How long can a fan take that pressure? After all, players get to retire. But fans go on and on, and after fifteen years of victory and being close to the greatest victory, San Franciscans may be tired, may even be ready to accept the cyclical nature of success and the need for a fallow period. We have six months to think about that, the off-season. But I know that on Saturday afternoon I felt tired enough to welcome the rest, no matter that being here for the 49ers' glory I count as one of my great pieces of luck in life.

England went back to their hotel in Hendon, and then they got in the team buses and were driven down to the Royal Garden Hotel on Kensington High Street for the official banquet and reception. There were celebrations all over England that night, a sense of national party. At the Royal Garden, the players were wined and dined while their wives and girlfriends were given a meal separately in another room. I've checked on this. You have to believe it and realise what a long time ago 1966 was and how primitive the society of sport can be. Let us add that to be married to a sportsman is likely one of the great travails of modern times.

Jimmy Greaves didn't go to the banquet.

The players, or some of them, went out on the town after the meal, and there were tales of immense drunkenness exploding the months of discipline and hard training. On the Sunday, the German party flew back to Frankfurt, where they were greeted by a huge crowd lining the drive from the airport to the city. The crowd chanted, 'You won all the same.' Also on the Sunday, a chauffeur-driven car containing Martin Peters was involved in a crash. Princess Alexandra had a daughter, and the England team for the upcoming Fourth Test against the West Indies at Headingly was announced. It was a fine team, and it was being thrashed by the West Indies:

Barber	Hunte
Boycott	Lashley
Milburn	Kanhai
Cowdrey	Butcher
Graveney	Nurse
D'Oliveira	Sobers
Parks	Holford
Titmus	Hendriks
Snow	Griffith
Higgs	Hall
Underwood	Gibbs

In the Monday papers, August 1st, it was reported that the BBC was busy filming an immense serialisation of John Galsworthy's *The Forsyte Saga*. Then on the Tuesday, there were reports from Austin, Texas that a seemingly harmless, ordinary young man named Whitman had first slaughtered all the members of his family and then climbed to the top of the tower that dominated the University of Texas campus and begun shooting at people.

The year unwound: in China, the Red Guards appeared, and their grim Cultural Revolution ensued; more troops were sent to Vietnam, and more died; Hendrik Verwoerd, Prime Minister of South Africa, was assassinated; Ronald Reagan was elected Governor of California; and late in the year, in Aberfan, Wales, a vast slag heap of coal dust, undermined by rains, collapsed on the village, and on its school, killing 28 adults and 116 children.

TIME AFTER TIME

In every team sport – and it is always team sport, I think, that moves fans the most – there are sequels, pay-backs and revenge. It should always be so, and in the moment of every victory and defeat the arc of continuity should be recalled, for it makes victors humble and losers hopeful. So Chelsea and Arsenal, say, play twice a year, every year; and the Dallas Cowboys and the 49ers know that they stand in each other's way on the road to the Super Bowl. Or they do so until such a time that one of the clubs becomes less than an obstacle.

England went on under Alf Ramsey. On January 1st, 1967, the Queen made him Sir Alf – she had to meet him – and in the same Honours List Bobby Moore got the OBE. Alf asked the players not to call him 'Sir Alf', and not to let anything get in the way of their relationship! Bobby Moore kept the old, polite grin on his face when he was with Alf. It had been Bobby who quietly frosted Alf after the West German victory when the FA awarded £22,000 to the squad as a bonus. Alf worked out a complex sliding scale so that people were rewarded according to the games they had played. Then Bobby and the others said, balls to that, a thousand pounds a man. And they all refused to declare the money for tax.

In the years between the World Cups of 1966 and 1970, Ramsey's England had a distinguished record:

4–2

P   35
W   21
D   10
L   4
GF   62
GA   22

Their only defeats were at the hands of Scotland (at Wembley in 1967), West Germany (away, 1–0), Brazil (in Rio, 2–1) and Yugoslavia (in Italy, 2–1, in the semi-final of the European Nations Cup).

For the 1970 World Cup, in Mexico, Ramsey said we would win again – it was that or we would turn into swans in the Mexican mid-day sun. But it was a reasonable prediction: the loss in Rio had been close, Ramsey's defence was still the basis of the team – only 22 goals given away in 35 games. And he was confident that he could build on the '66 team for the next World Cup.

In fact, the 22-man squad for Mexico kept eight of the winning team from '66 – only Cohen, Wilson and Hunt were gone. As newcomers, Alf included Keith Newton and Terry Cooper as full-backs, Alan Mullery and Colin Bell in midfield, as well as Francis Lee and Peter Osgood up front. But this was now entirely a squad without wingers. Thus, the great stress Alf put upon running – of midfield players and full-backs becoming wingers from time to time – would be maintained no matter that one of the threats for England in the Mexico tournament was playing in the heat and humidity while still running the Ramsey way. But there was a new opportunity in this World Cup: a limited number of substitutes would be allowed.

I think that overall 1970's is the best team England has ever had in a World Cup. Moore, Hurst and Ball were all better players than in 1966, though Hurst never found those story-book passages again. Even playing 4–4–2 in the heat, this was a very skilled and experienced side.

In their first game, they beat Romania, 1–0, thanks to a Hurst goal. Then they had to play Brazil: it was a qualifying match, yet it always felt like a final. The match was played in Guadalajara, with kick-off at noon (to please European TV audiences). The temperature was nearly 100 degrees, which is no weather for soccer the way England played it. The line-up was as follows:

Banks

Wright   Labone   Moore   Cooper

Mullery   Ball   B. Charlton   Peters

Lee   Hurst

O

Paulo Cesar   Pelé   Tostão   Jairzinho

Clodoaldo   Rivelino

Everaldo   Piazza   Brito   Carlos Alberto

Felix

Wright was deputizing for the injured Keith Newton. But Brazil had a greater loss: Gerson was hurt, and replaced by Paulo Cesar.

It was an extraordinary match, and maybe the best England ever managed. After ten minutes, Banks made the save from Pelé, moving across the face of his goal, instinctively knocking a great downwards header up and over the bar. England made and missed chances. Mullery marked Pelé as well as anyone could. Moore never played better. But still after sixty minutes, Brazil scored through Jairzinho. Alf used substitutes: he replaced Lee with Jeff Astle, and Bobby Charlton with Colin Bell – Bobby by then was thirty-three, and Alf wanted to rest him for future games. Ball hit the bar, but we lost, 1–0. After the game, Pelé said that he reckoned Banks and Moore were without equals at their positions. It was still possible for the two sides to meet again, in the Final.

We beat Czechoslovakia, 1–0, so we qualified, with Brazil, from what had been a very tough group. And so, in the quarter-finals, at León, on Sunday June 14th, we were set to meet West Germany. The line-up was this:

Bonetti

Newton   Labone   Moore   Cooper

Ball   Mullery   B. Charlton   Peters

Lee   Hurst

O

Libuda   Muller   Löhr

Seeler   Overath   Beckenbauer

Höttges   Fichtel   Vogts   Schnellinger

Maier

Bobby Charlton, Schnellinger and Seeler were in their fourth World Cup, though Bobby never actually played in 1958. Moore was in his third. Schulz was there again as a German reserve. But the most vital piece of team news was that Banks was sick to his stomach after a bottle of Mexican beer and so had to be replaced by Chelsea's Peter Bonetti. Beckenbauer was a great player by now, and this is the match in which he and Moore gazed at one another across the field as immaculate peers.

There were stories in advance that one or two English players would play the first half as if that's all there was – and then be substituted, so as to get the best use out of fresh legs. But that wasn't really in Alf's nature. Still, for a solid hour, England were magnificent. Mullery was never better, and his goal after thirty minutes was in the tradition of the last one England had scored against this side, Hurst's third at Wembley. In the second half, as Schulz came on for Höttges, England scored again, through

Peters – that was one of his few golden moments in 1970.

2–0 up with forty minutes to play. Alf was about to put Bell on in place of Charlton, when Beckenbauer scored – eventually, he was going to score. Though this was a poor effort, and it would not have been a goal but for Bonetti's ghastly error. Was Bonetti over-awed by the occasion? England tired. Beckenbauer expanded. With ten minutes to go an awkward back-header from Seeler looped over Bonetti's head – he was out of position again. 2–2. In the extra time, Gerd Muller scored the winning goal. England were gone.

West Germany were beaten by Italy, who then lost, 4–1, to a Brazil with Gerson restored in the Final. In hindsight, I don't think England could have held Brazil as close again. They'd have been exhausted by the Final, and Alf seemed unwilling to use Osgood with any confidence. So England's failure was blamed on the Chelsea goalkeeper. And surely Banks would have kept the Germans out, enough for us to get to the semi-finals.

No-one could foresee it then, but this was the end of an era for England. In so many ways, English and British soccer were at their peak in the years after 1966. Celtic beat Inter-Milan in the European Cup in 1967. And then next year, in the same competition, Manchester United beat Benfica, 4–1, in the Final at Wembley – and without Denis Law, who was injured! That night was the final vindication for United, Matt Busby and Bobby Charlton, and it was a great team:

Stepney

Brennan   Dunne

Crerand   Foulkes   Stiles

Best   Kidd   Charlton   Sadler   Aston

The emotion of that victory, and the sense of Munich's dead being honoured at last, was extraordinary. But the loveliest moment of a spectacular game was when Eusébio went clear with only Stepney to beat. Somehow, at point-blank range, Stepney saved and in a daze hurled the ball away. Eusébio was amazed and moved, and instead of retreating he wanted to shake Stepney's hand. But the keeper was in the zone, and he couldn't see the chivalry, so Eusébio smiled and shrugged and went on with the game.

And then Chelsea had another of their moments. In 1970, they got to the Cup Final, against the loathed and deeply feared Leeds. The game at Wembley was brutal and harsh. The two sides felt honest enmity, and Leeds were still Bremner-Charlton-Hunter in defence. Chelsea had a side of huge craft and lazy, big-head genius, but we had our hard men: Harris and Webb, for two. It went for a replay, at Old Trafford, and Chelsea won.

Bonetti

Webb   McCreadie

Hollins   Hinton   Harris

Cooke   Hudson   Osgood   Hutchinson   Houseman

The following year, we beat Real Madrid and won the Cup Winners' Cup. Then Chelsea went to sleep again, suffered relegation, and only just got back into the Premier League in time. It's about time for glory again.

As for England, well . . . put it this way. In the seven World Cups that have followed 1966, West Germany have qualified for the Finals on all seven occasions. They have won twice – in 1974, in Germany, when Beckenbauer was captain; and then again, in 1990, in Italy, when Beckenbauer managed the side. In addition, they were beaten finalists twice, a semi-finalist once, and in the quarter-finals on the other two occasions. That is a terrific, professional, abiding record and a tribute to the quality of German League soccer, as well as the German sense of winning.

The English League was once as powerful – and may be still. For in the years we're considering, England had the great teams of Manchester United, Liverpool and Nottingham Forest (under Brian Clough). But in those seven Cups, England were a semi-finalist once, and a quarter-finalist three times. On three occasions, however – in '74, '78 and '94 – they did not even qualify for the Finals. This is no place to go into those failures, or the succession of managers. Let me just say that there were ways in which England's victory in 1966 made later defeats a little more likely, and a little more excusable for the players.

TIME OUT

This has been a book about one match – granted the asides and diversions – spelled out in what may seem inordinate, excruciating, detail. But I wanted to show that one two-hour contest might be like an epic poem, a saga, or a legendary performance. Still, as I wrote, studying the none-too-fine tape of the match, striving to be accurate, I knew my feelings were creeping in – as you have probably decided, I like Bobby Moore and Beckenbauer, and I am mystified by Hunt and Peters playing so much for England. You have your own favourites. No matter that a game happened, and may be reassembled from all the camera angles, it is your dream, your game. I know that I have always needed sports in the way I want movies – my other, but no stronger, passion – as fuel for fantasizing. And I'm not sure how healthy fantasizing is.

For decades, for instance, I've had this day-dream about the 1966 World Cup. It's come to my aid on sleepless nights and trudging through the snow to dreaded meetings. We are ten minutes or so into the second half of the quarter-finals: it is England against anyone, but our opponents have just gone 2-0 up. The game is at Wembley and the crowd is turning ugly. Then the camera – for somehow my fantasies do not run or play, except as movies – zooms down to find a worried-looking Ramsey on the touchline, about to make a substitution. (This is an advantage he never had in 1966, of course.) He is going to take Hunt or Peters out and bring in this dark, somewhat overweight, rather shaggy-haired rebel – a great but moody player he has never trusted or much liked. This is the crisis, and Ramsey is conceding a kind of defeat. Waiting for a natural stoppage in the game, Alf is nattering on to the player about what to do and the player is ostentatiously not attending.

This player is a version of Jimmy Greaves, but he is Len Shackleton, too, Peter Osgood, Charlie George, Stan Bowles, Rodney Marsh, Glen Hoddle. He is every erratic ball-playing 'genius' there ever was who regarded dogged work-rate soccer with scorn. And he is me.

The stoppage comes, the substitute is on. But as he steps on to the field, he takes out his false teeth and drops them in Alf's startled hand. He then goes on and generates a 4–2 victory with the greatest thirty-five minutes of soccer artistry anyone has ever seen.

I will be fifty-five by the time this book is published, and I'm not sure whether it is more indecent and ridiculous to be having that day-dream still, or to be admitting to it in print. Let me go further with it. This player – who effectively won the Cup in 1966 – retired from the game and went to live in America. To be a writer.

Then came the day, in 1994, when the nations agreed to stage a World Cup in the United States of America (once, that would have been as lurid and demented a fantasy as this one of mine). England qualified, another fond hope, and the new manager, Terry Venables, astonished the nation by naming this fifty-three-year-old once-great to the squad. After all, says El Tel, 'Stanley Matthews was playing at fifty, and I think David can still give us a useful twenty minutes.' Well . . . well, you can imagine how it turns out.

I have a hunch that nearly everyone who goes to football has this kind of thriving, secret, insane lust for glory. And if *you* don't, I'd be grateful if you kept the point to yourself.

I never knew how to ask my Dad whether he had such dreams. There was no way of getting that close to him. In the end, what I most loathed about him, or was most afraid of, was that there was no talking about intimate and ridiculous things. And I know that the only chance I had of getting near him was through sport – in holding that catch, or being there with him when, incredibly, Tooting took a 2–0 lead.

My mother died in the summer of 1976. I had come back from one year in America with a family that had broken up because of my recklessness, and my infliction of damage. Marriages are two people, of course, but I had made the decision, and I take the responsibility. I left my wife and three children. And I went back to America to be with the woman, Lucy, who is my wife now.

My Dad handled my mother's death as gracelessly as I might have imagined. My mother's illness and the funeral were grisly, not least because of his attempt to act as if nothing was happening. We had more angry exchanges than ever before, but he was oddly tender about my broken marriage, and he even suggested that I simply take the children off to America with me. But he also refused to invite me to St Albans to see his other life and to meet his other 'wife'. I gathered later that he believed I might have made a scene – which was a fair guess. But I felt that he was curiously upstaged by what I was doing, and by the openness about it.

There were several years in which the kids came to America in the summer, and I came back to England in the winter. Years in which Mathew and I went to see Chelsea at the Bridge and the Red Sox at Fenway Park. And for a while, at least, I was following five sports, enjoying Trevor Francis and Larry Bird, John Snow and Carl Yastrzemski, from month to month.

English football dismayed me more and more – or was I gradually becoming American? I had mixed feelings about Alf Ramsey, like nearly everyone who knew his time in charge. And Alf laid up his enemies and his fate, like a New Englander stacking logs for the winter. But he had succeeded with the greatest personal modesty and the least thought of reward. When he was eventually discarded as manager of England, he was earning a fraction of what noisier club managers were paid. And now, apparently, outrageously, he is no hero. No matter that he did what no other manager has done.

But English soccer suffered from his success. The stress on defence, on work and fitness – all sensible, all admirable – left the game less of a spectacle. Then the English fans failed to live up to the 'challenge' of having black players enter the game. There were shameful chants against those players, so wretched as to kill the game's pleasure. That was only a part of the mounting violence at soccer in England, the sense that some people were going to the games only to make trouble.

I will not attempt to analyse that. Britain was in hard, changing times in the late 1970s, and then under Margaret Thatcher it was given bitter medicine that left many young males feeling useless and alienated. Maybe there was less violence on the pitch – for the game had become less physical, less rough – and so there had to be more in the crowd. Maybe the small Fascist element proved more effective at provoking disorder than ever they have managed in other arenas of British political life. Maybe winning the World Cup, and the increasing exposure to Continental sides, had made Englishmen more xenophobic and worse losers.

Of course, finally, there were the three disasters that changed the game, or how one felt about it: the riot at Heysel Stadium in Brussels, the European Cup Final of 1985, Liverpool v. Juventus, when 39 people died in mayhem set off by English supporters; the fire at Bradford Stadium; and the panic or the frenzy on the terraces at Hillsborough in 1989 with 95 men and boys crushed.

There had been disasters at soccer grounds before, when a huge crowd in an enclosed space took fright, like cattle outside an abattoir: in 1946, 33 people were killed at Bolton Wanderers; and there were tragedies at Ibrox Stadium in Glasgow, in 1902 and 1971. I have described being in a crowd at Stamford Bridge as a kid when there was danger in the air. But the men there then were so eager to be protective. By the 1970s, there was a feeling of poised violence that only made panic more likely. And so the game has been, sensibly, reformed. Grounds now are devoid of terraces or standing-room. Everyone sits and feels safer. The ticket prices have shot up. The crowds are, by necessity, much smaller. You can never stand in the awesome mass of strangers again and be moved by their gentle power.

The country is more disturbed and disordered now, and surely that's the result of processes that started in the 1960s and had to begin – things like sex and violence, the overthrow of stale order and habit – the search for liberty, and the readiness to talk about fantasy, divorce and double lives.

Eventually, I met my father's other 'wife' – her name was Anne – and he even married her in 1984. In all the waiting, she had acquired a strange glamour: she must be a love match, I reckoned, a dark, fatalistic, profound woman who somehow loved my Dad so much she could stand his being away. It was not so. She proved to be a bitter little Lancastrian woman, like someone out of *Coronation Street*. And by the time I met her, she seemed to wish that my Dad would be away much more. When I had let a few years go by and got over the fear of rushing to judgment, I reached the conclusion that she was as nasty and petty as anyone I've ever met. And not worthy of him. I had the terrible fear that fifty years or so ago – they had been together since 1944 – he had made a mistake, and then despaired of changing his life, of seeking more, of wanting to win. Perhaps he came home so often because he never quite owned up to her in his own mind.

This is a narrow book in one way, just one match; yet in another, it's expansive, about all of sport. I thought of ending as Hemingway ended *Death in the Afternoon*, with a chapter that starts, 'If I could have made this enough of a book it would have had everything in it.'

Then I might have passed quickly over so many small things that seemed so wondrous at the time: the living dream of Hurst's last shot going into the net; the mischief in Larry Bird's face and the knowledge that he was whispering trash in other players' ears; the wriggle in George Best and then the straightening as he shot; the horror when Bobby Moore died so young; Pasarell against Gonzales, Stan Smith against Nastase, Maria Bueno and Margaret Court; Barry Bonds homering as if the ball were destined and he was simply tracing its path with his bat; realising how far Bob Beamon had jumped and knowing there could be no trick, only some amazing interference with nature; and going down to Fenway once with Mathew, driving from Vermont, and passing through a rain storm so fierce that driving was folly, but going on, and getting to a dry Boston and the snooker-table grass, and seeing Dwight Evans – Mathew's favourite player – come out of a slump with two homers.

Fathers and sons at the game. On May 29th 1995 I took Nicholas, who was five then, to the Oakland Coliseum to see the Athletics play the Red Sox. It was Memorial Day – the day on which America remembers the dead in all its wars. Before the afternoon game began, the colours were presented, shots were fired in the air by the Colour Guard, and three World War II planes flew overhead. Then a frail, elderly man with white hair, and wearing a dark suit, walked out to the mound to throw out the first pitch.

It was Joe DiMaggio, who was eighty then and who, in the summer of 1941, hit safely in 56 games in a row. He then had a hitless game in Cleveland. But came back and hit in another 16 in a row. In other words, he didn't relax. Oh sure, he had a career batting average of .325 and he married Marilyn Monroe, and he was about the only man in her life who never took advantage of her or said a bad word about her. He was one of the greatest players; and he was elegant and he was shy. And Nicholas got to see him that once and listened patiently as I talked about him, and for days thereafter he called him Joe DiMagic.

And he'd better not forget. Because, if he has grandchildren, and he and a grandchild are lucky enough in their time to have a game, or a match, that matters, really matters, why, it is likely that DiMaggio's 56-game streak – or, rather, his way of life – will have happened a hundred years ago.

This book had its origins in a conversation between my agent, Laura Morris, and David Reynolds of Bloomsbury. I am so grateful to them for having the idea, and thinking of me; and then for being such friends and supporters of the game itself.

There are several other people who helped: David Thompson (not a misprint), who got me BBC tapes of old games; Mark Feeney, who read the text and offered sound advice and invaluable corrections; Sean Arnold and Mathew Thomson, who consulted and argued; the Minet Library, in South London, that had valuable archives; Greil Marcus and Fred Stout, who had good points to make; Tim de Lisle, himself a fine sports writer; Tom Rosenthal, for cricket information; and Lorraine Latorraca, who typed as fast as I could write, and who became interested in how the strange match would end.

But, as must be clear from the book itself, the greatest thanks go to family members.